PERSONAL EXISTENCE
AFTER DEATH

PERSONAL EXISTENCE AFTER DEATH

Reductionist Circularities and the Evidence

Robert J. Geis

Sherwood Sugden & Company
PUBLISHERS
315 5th Street, Peru, Illinois 61354

FIRST EDITION

Sherwood Sugden & Company, Publishers
315 Fifth Street
Peru, Illinois 61354

Printed and bound in the United States of America.

ISBN 0-89385-044-6

CONTENTS

Introduction

What follows is an empirical inquiry into the proposition "Man is immortal." Presumably the study of empirical data is truth-giving. A study of such data in the absence of assumptions which need to be proved is desirable. One which begins with evidence accessible to anyone willing to consider it possesses an appeal, one would think, that makes for a promising approach to any area of puzzlement in the human sciences. If that is granted, the approach taken here may place in more than a modest doubt the current fashion, materialism. Man is nothing but flesh that death returns to earth is its view, briefly stated. For that view, there is no evidentiary basis. The materialist position, as will become obvious in the course of reviewing it, stems from assumptions that beg the question. That will mean what materialism advances for its assertion is not evidence at all.

An attentive consideration to the evidence that functioning in the world, the here and now, provides, suggests quite a contrary position to materialism. Attentiveness to empirical data—activities and operations of everyday human existence—makes a persuasive case that man may indeed be immortal.

What this book attempts to do is to present those data in coherent manner to show how evidence from everyday human functioning suggests the credibility of human immortality. While religious systems all at one time or another have offered immortality as a belief, this book does not present their case. An empirical inquiry—a concentration only on the merits at hand—should not invoke religious beliefs as evidence. Those beliefs do not meet the tests of evidence that an empirical study of immortality requires. Nor, for that reason, have we looked into the moral claims for immortality. Those arguments, too, seem to lack the rigor required for an empirical approach. The road toward certainty, it seems to me, is an empirical one.

The data this book addresses are (1) the operations of human thought processes, operations that are familiar to everyone and in which everyone shares. We experience these operations daily—moment to moment, in fact, in daily living. That qualifies them as empirical data: events and realities most immediate to us. Beginning with these we look to see where they lead us in the resolution of the immorality debate. Put otherwise, this undertaking does not begin with a theory of these operations and seek to fit the immortality question into the framework of that theory. Vaporous theory asserting endless existence is of no help in studying man's final moments on earth. Instead, we begin with the data as they present themselves to us and the conclusions they subsequently encourage.

Looking next at (2) neurophysiological data—the physical workings of the human brain—furthers the empirical study. We can, however tedious the inquiry into those data becomes, focus on how those workings of the brain advance or detract from the claim that man exists beyond death. A dispassionate and analytical approach to them has much merit, and that has been attempted here. The evidence of the inner mechanisms of man's brain, when subjected to a sufficiently critical reflection, will advance the claim for the survivability of the human person.

Beyond these two sets of empirical, recognizable, data lies an examination of the near-death, out-of-body experience. Clearly it qualifies as an empirical basis for study, given the widespread reports of such claimed events in the literature today. A protracted and careful examination of these events is requisite in any approach to the question of man's immortality. It will be argued that one can dismiss such events only on the most inadequate grounds. What truth-giving data this event provides will enlarge our understanding of man's potential for existence. Those data will make available further reflections on what additional issues are pertinent when personhood is beyond death. The theory of reincarnation becomes a topic, accordingly, in this regard. Its shortcomings are then suggested, as well as those of so-called neurophilosophy. Its criticism of "folk psychology"—everyday language's separation of mental from neurological, cognitive from biological—will evince more a shortcoming of neurophilosophic tenets than any inadequacy they claim in common speech's descriptions of man as a thinking versus neurally-complex active organism. In this matter, we shall reason, everyday discourse has achieved a refinement of expression that correctness of thought always carries with it.

That is the overall plan of discussion. It is probably accurate to comment that the standards of evidence set in this work for the cogency of arguments against immortality are the same that opponents of immortality have set for the proponents of it. So setting them is a desirable procedure if any value is to be given to the notion of balance and symmetry. It is one to which most subscribe.

There is no pretense to elegance of expression. And flights of fancy have hopefully been avoided. The book is perhaps best viewed as a brief harnessing datum and evidence for a claim that evidence shows is not easy to rebut. The claim is that a denial of human immortality is unsubstantiated, and that from what lived experience and our everyday human operations tells us its assertion is perhaps closer to the truth than those issues we have come to think are.

I
Evidence and Certainty

Extinction. Life has ended and the long-feared disintegration of your body has begun. Finished: everything you are is gone. All striving was for nought. Destroyed. You are finished. You have become decomposing shreds of thinning tissue. Consciousness has run out. At the moment of death all the movement of existence is emptied. Nothing exists anymore. You have ceased to be.

The bodily dissolution that has frightened you is the end of all your capabilities. Unlike your sleep, this time awareness does not return. Lying in the hospital bed, you know this is the moment you have always dreaded. Caught in the round of crossfire, you drop into blackness. As the waves engulf you in their undertow, the car plunges into the ditch below, the searing swordlike pain rips into your chest, death comes, and you are no more. Whatever you are simply vanishes. Your life is over. Between two boundless nights your life was a momentary pulse of a light that could not last. It is extinguished.

At the end, you do not even remain a bit of bone. You become indistinguishable from the earth. At the last gasp of breath you have lost. The wars you have waged—with others and with yourself—amount to nothing. Death has bludgeoned them into wasted effort. What memories come to mind as you breathe your very last? A useless question. Your existence is over.

Is it not the case that the total and unconditional end of the man is sealed with the death certificate? Such is one common notion of death. Interment in the tomb is one's last, and utterly passive, act. Once the brain no longer functions, what else is there to life? Without the brain, consciousness stops. Our awareness of self, of others, of the world, stops. If a blow to the head impairs our functioning, then what effect would complete damage to the brain tissue have? Is it not by the restoration of injured parts, through the healing process, that a body reverses negative effects?

Without this healing process, our ability to be in the world would greatly decline. If this is the case, in the absence of healing, what happens in the event of death?

The importance of this question requires that we examine, in detail, how the mind comes to an answer. Those asserting that death is finality are obviously laying claim to a truth in that assertion. Examining their reasoning will be of value, because, unfounded assumptions and circularity of reasoning shall appear that are at the base of assertions against endless personhood.

The point merits repeating. Claims and arguments rejecting immortality, when carefully considered, show themselves not to meet the standards of proof and evidence that cogency demands. What appear to be firm foundations for such arguments do not bear up to scrutiny. Meticulous and attentive examination, which any search for truth necessitates, will make that plain. Care and precision of argument are requirements given the seriousness of the issue we are addressing: the status of post-mortem man. Once the arguments against immortality are seen to be, as we claim, inconclusive, then core and precision of argument will enable us to start on a sure footing when presenting evidence which, we will argue, does not suffer from the weaknesses which the assertions against immortality do.

We come to conclusions about questions we have through the use of evidence. Evidence puts an end to inquiry in that in its absence, inquiry would continue. In this way, whatever brings inquiry to an end is called evidence. If an end to inquiry signifies the acquisition of knowledge, then evidence is what promotes knowledge. In the presence of evidence, that about which we inquire has been answered.[1]

What evidence do we have that at death individual personhood is destroyed? What kind of evidence may we ask for in this regard? What licenses someone to assert that at death personhood is extinguished? That bodily death is equivalent to personal death? Is the evidence presented for this assertion adequate? Could man have come to an after-life notion without the actual reality of an after-life? Or is the notion some metaphorical variant of awakening from sleep, and nothing more? Is it a postulate impelled by the fear of death? Is not the case against an after-life so overwhelming that tenacious belief in it amounts to delusion?

Surveying the different kinds of evidence available to inquiry ought to provide a weighed resolution to this question. Evidence is whatever goes towards resolving a question that has arisen in the mind. It is what brings the question to rest: certainty.

At first look, certainty seems to admit of degrees: one subject matter permits a greater certainty than another. The most obvious illustration of this is a comparison of the certainty achieved in geometry as opposed to that in moral matters. In Euclidean space[2] the shortest distance between two points—both in theory and fact—is a straight line. That is indisputably the case. A fixed fact alterable only by a change in the structure of three-dimensional existence, the space that we know. As long as three-dimensionality remains what we, from both theory and experience, know it to be, there can be no uncertainty about the claim made for a straight line. The issue is closed.

In matters of right, or appropriate, conduct, our certainty is not so clearly set. In the lived circumstance—the material for moral judgments—certainty as to what specific action in a situation advances moral well-being, is often elusive. The always shifting conditions of human action do not provide for universality about any particular course of action. The uniformity necessary for the sameness of conclusion about any action is lacking. Particular rules of conduct do not have the evidentiary backing found in those of the propositions of geometry. Absent that backing, certitude about what action is most proportioned to a good end or result is not on the level furnished by the evidence in geometry. Our certainty is enough, though, that we render punishment through courts of law for actions deemed morally wrong.

These are, then, two avenues of certainty. In moral matters, frequently the evidence leaves room for doubt about the judgments we make in particular circumstances, however certain we are of the general moral truth that applies. In cases of geometrical reasoning, a proposition is perceived, without question, to be true. It is indubitable. Unlike moral matters, certain corollaries regarding it can be adduced with indubitability. The mind immediately locates a necessity flowing through geometrical properties one to the other. The reason for such certainty is the unalterability of geometrical propositions.[3] In geometry, we encounter evidence that we grasp immediately as unarguable, in virtue of that very evidence. It is irreducible, not further analyzable. It is so basic that it cannot be questioned. The evidence providing for geometrical reasoning is apprehended as always

sure, never differing. For this reason, when we think geometrical-
ly, if we reach a stage that does not have the necessity we know
geometry to have, we can be certain we have proceeded incor-
rectly. For the nature of geometrical evidence does not allow
anything less than necessary judgments.

This way of necessity and indubitability is not the only basis for
claiming knowledge. Other areas of study do not proceed by way
of the certainty seen in mathematical science. They are not
possessed of its kind of evidence. Some certainties are immediately indubitable. We cannot question them. To others, however,
we must reason. In that way, the certainty is derived. That,
however, does not detract from the certainty we reach through
such reasoning. Such certainty is caused by premises that individually are prehended as true and certain. Conjoined in thought,
the conclusion resulting from that conjunction has the same
force of indubitability as the statements we saw in geometry.
Truths reached by a process of premisses, in an argument-form
known as the syllogism, lack only an immediate indubitability.
They can be doubted when taken in isolation from the premisses
leading up to them. However, as a product of the conjunction in
thought of premisses prehended as true and certain, they cannot
be doubted. The evidence in the premisses that generated them
show doubt to be a rejection of what is the case, and the denial of
any truth so generated to be a denial of what is true.[4]

Therefore, in the sort of proof we are seeking in the question
of immortal existence, it does not detract from our reasoning
about it should certainty about immortality result from a series of
premises in an argument. To think that it does is to assume that
certainty is best when underived, when not arrived at through
premises, but holding only in virtue of the terms or notes
involved in that certainty. But there is no evidence for such an assumption. Nor is it intuitively clear that evidence is strongest this
way, or any stronger than that which is a conclusion reached in
reasoning from premises.

The certainty in reasoning through premisses differs from the
certainty in geometry in that in geometry the certainty is
immediate because of the evidence supplied. We do not reason to
it. In other situations, as with reasoning about human immortality, the certainty is called mediated. There is no one piece of
evidence that gives us the underived certitude of mathematical
propositions. The evidence, instead, comes in steps. After a suffi-

cient number of steps that the evidence leads to has been taken, we are led to that conclusion to which the evidence shows those steps to have led us. When those steps, those premisses of an argument that the evidence allows, show themselves to be connected, one inextricably to the other—whatever the area of study might be—our certainty is no less than that of geometry. In neither instance can we deny the evidence without contradicting what the evidence shows to be indubitable. Thus, while the certainty we have through premisses of an argument is reached differently than the certainty of a proposition that is immediately indubitable (as, e.g., the type that we saw in geometry), it does not differ in degree from the immediate certainty. The conclusion reached in the syllogism whose premisses are true and certain is of no less value or probity than a statement or proposition that is known without argument or reasoning to be true. In denying such a conclusion, we are involved in the same kind of contradiction that would occur in denying a proposition or statement that was true without the need for premisses to show that it was true.

What certainty, accordingly, do we find in the data offered as proof against survival? On the most basic level, opponents of post-mortem survival cite the corpse as their evidence for denial. All signs of human life are absent, and that, they hold, is evidentiary grounds for certainty.

There is an assumption here that is gratuitous. The denial assumes, requires, post-mortem survival means life as it appears to us in our present state. The assumption is that, to survive death, is to exist the same way we exist in this life; that if we do not exist in death the way we did in life, we do not survive death. Said otherwise, the denial requires that we assume that whatever is human is restricted to this world of flesh-and-bone interaction. There can be nothing human, it is being assumed, that is not on this level. Anything not of this nature of material experience cannot be human. It is being assumed that human existence—everything that is human—has to be constrained to this life. To how life is experienced in our current state. Obviously, under such constraints, human existence could not continue after this life because that possibility has already been ruled out by what this denial of survivability has assumed: Existence as it is in this life is all there is to being human. That if existence beyond death is not life as we know it, then personhood ceases at death. And, since in the grave life as we know it clearly does not take place, existence for any one human has ended.

On what grounds are these statements made? What data for them qualify as evidence? They are not statements whose terms make them self-evident. The claim, i.e., is not obvious on the face of it. There is nothing intrinsic to, or inherent in, the meaning of the terms that compels us to equate "human existence" with "life in this world." Denying that the two are equated is not contradictory.

Proof through a series of premisses is necessary, if the assumption: "anything not part of, not restricted to, this life is not human," is to have any force of persuasion. Any assertion not true on its own merits requires evidence that takes the form of premisses conjoined in thought to exhibit its truth. This is how an argument is conducted when a claim is not immediately evident. Claims evident of themselves need no such argumentation. They are inarguable.

There are, though, no premisses we could use for proof of the assumption that already do not presuppose what has to be proven. The opponents of post-mortem survival assume, as we have seen, an identity between human life (life as it appears, takes place, in this world) and human existence. The identification of human existence with this life would require, for purposes of proof, the general proposition: "In every living being, life and existence are the same," or, equivalently; "Whatever lives, *exists*, only insofar as it lives." So that, "The end of life is the end of existence," could follow. We know directly that there is a difference between life and existence.[5] But in this case, the opponents of post-mortem survival have equated the two. Their assumption, then, is "To live is to have an existence that ends with life." There is nothing, however, about life that tells us this is so. If what is true of the set is true of its members, it follows that there is nothing about human life (a member of the set 'life') that tells us that existence as a human ends with life as a human.

Is there a chain of thinking, on the other hand, in which truths properly ordered, not in a causal way, but in a relationship of priority only, establish mortality as a certainty? In such an ordering, one truth follows upon another in the sense that it could not be known without a prior truth being known. In geometry, e.g., I cannot declare the formula for finding the diagonal of the square without first knowing a triangle's properties. The latter does not cause the former the way premisses cause a conclusion. But my knowledge of the former is subsequent upon, and assured by, the truth of the latter. In this ordering, one truth is more primarily known, and more basic. Subsequent truths are related to it as the more complex is to the simpler, and prehended clearly as so related.

This is the way mathematics proceeds: with rigor, clarity, and certainty. And once mathematics had great favor in the history of ideas as the method for all inquiry. Surely such a method, where knowledge increases from one certainty ordered to another, is worth examining in the claim that man is mortal. Can this claim be asserted the way truths in mathematics are? In this procedure, one would not ask what generates the assertion "Man is mortal." That is the procedure of the syllogism. The method of mathematics directs we find what truth is more primarily known, without which a subsequent truth in the expansion of knowledge could not be known. So situated, that truth would arise as properly ordered and fixed in the chain of human reasoning.

Accordingly, to what truth could the assertion of human mortality be connected that is more primarily known and basic? And on what knowledge would the mortality assertion be an advance? What truth would follow upon it without which that truth could not be known?

This means that first we must see what truth is simpler, in the order of discovery, than the truth of the claim; "Man is mortal." In the order of mathematics, a simpler figure is chosen about whose truths we discourse before proceeding to a more complex figure, as we saw in the case of the square and the triangle. In the case of man, we cannot do this, because, doing so assumes man is a being derived from, or composed of, simpler beings, less complex entities. And of this, certainty is non-existent. The human body is composed of simpler constituents—cells, e.g., which in turn are comprised of proteins. That is not the same as saying man is comprised only of his constituents. For that, man and body would have to be identical. For this, no conceptualization is compelling. Empirically, there is no incontrovertible case for the identification. And nothing in our concept of man carries with it the note, "mortal being." Denying the two are necessarily conjoined, is not contradictory. Assuming, to the contrary, that there was evidence of man's derivation from simpler beings, the order of mathematical thinking would require that we see incontrovertibly how, in this ordering, immortality, as a property of man, would be excluded. Dissimilarity of sides in geometric figures rules out congruence of their angles. This is indisputable, and is known subsequent to the rules of intersection. Immortal existence and human personhood are not mutually exclusive in the way that exclusion of properties are known in mathematics. Nor are mortality and human personhood mutually inclusive in that way. The order of mathematics, and its route to certainty, cannot show that man is mortal.

In two methods for reaching knowledge, then—one by way of premises, the other, an ordering of incontrovertible truths by way of their priority—no evidence making mortality, a certainty has appeared. Our sense-knowledge, it may be averred, gives us no evidence that a lifeless body exhibits any characteristics resembling personhood. And on this alone, the contention might continue, we can argue that at death a person ceases to exist. If sense-data, from which all human knowledge originates, present nothing resembling human life, can we not conclude with certitude that the matter is closed?

We could, if all the data about what it means to be human allowed the same conclusion that our sense-perception of a lifeless corpse allowed. If there were no evidence to the contrary, then clearly we would be justified in saying that, so far as we know, given just the matter of a lifeless corpse, death is the extinction, whole and entire, of human personhood.

There are, though, facets of a person's life not open to sensory awareness. And since this is so, then not all the data about being human are accessible to sense-awareness. That means that sensory awareness does not tell us everything about a human being. From this it follows that whatever a lifeless corpse indicated to sense-perception, however it appeared to our sense-awareness, it does not mean that what appears to us in such an instance to be the case, is the case.

Certainly the corpse is non-moving, and all signs of awareness to sensory stimuli are absent. To conclude from this extinction of personhood is to implicitly assume, however, that personhood is constituted by movement and awareness to sensory stimuli. In the absence of evidence either contradicting or weakening that assumption, at best we could only conclude that we cannot be sure that at death personhood is destroyed. The reason for the lack of certainty is plain. We are assuming some- thing in that judgment for which no evidence can be marshalled: we cannot prove that personhood is identical with movement and sensory stimuli awareness.

In this very important line of reasoning opponents of immortality might grant that, true, sensory awareness does not prehend all that is constitutive of personhood. No one can have sense-perception of my thoughts; no one can experience my particular pains, joys, or view- point of the world except me. My view of the world is intrinsically unique, as is every conscious being's. Surely, though, the argument may continue, are not my activities and movement in the world a result of my thoughts and sense-perceptions? And if bodily movement, movement occasioned by consciousness of the world and the thoughts I have, ends, is it not a sound inference to hold that thought and consciousness end also?

It would be, if all thought or awareness caused movement, if the two were necessarily conjoined, if they entailed each other. There is no evidence, though, neither from the terms involved nor from observation that this is so. Arguing, on the other hand, that thought processes would be impossible without bodily activity is to assert that bodily processes are necessary to cognitive processes. Which is to argue circularly; it is to argue that thought in the absence of bodily conditions is impossible. And that is precisely what is to be proven. Brain death, on these grounds, also cannot be adduced as proof of personal extinction. One would have to demonstrate that one's thought was the product of brain processes. More precisely, that in the absence of the brain, thought would be impossible; and that cannot be proven.

Taking this enumeration of alternatives against the assertion of immortality to be exhaustive, there is no evidence one can cite, then, ruling out the possibility of individual immortality. The assertion that man is mortal, when examined closely, points to assumptions that are either not evident on their own, or cannot be proven. Sensory awareness, our most immediate and direct contact with the world, offers no evidence making mortality a certainty. And in the two methods of reasoning which man employs to reach correct statements, through the syllogism or the order of mathematical theorems, no conjunction of premises or ordering of certainties tells us that man is mortal. And while thinking and brain processes can be related, the impossibility of thinking in the absence of a physical brain cannot be demonstrated. Such a demonstration would be necessary if one were to be at all convinced that brain death was the end, totally and irrevocably, of one's personhood.

Quite importantly, this allows us to examine the issue without the burden of dealing with claims that immortality simply is non-existent. The claims are without evidence, or simply incapable of a proof such a claim would require for what the issue demands.

We are entitled, then, to look for evidence that allows us to view immortality as (1) a possibility, (2) a probability, and (3) a certainty. A situation or entity is possible if it does not involve a contradiction. The order of existence—that order independent of our thought—precludes contradictoriness: self-contradictions are not realizable, are impossibilities. Whatever can exist, whatever can be realized, is not self-contradictory.

In the order of thought two terms in a statement are prehended as the same, incompatible, or as compatible. In the first the statement is uninformative, as in "A bachelor is someone who has no wife." The terms (the subject and predicate) are identical in meaning, and compatible. In statements whose terms are not the same but compatible, we think we have gained information from the statement. Any statement that communicates information is of this type. A statement in which the terms being related are incompatible with each other involves us in an impossibility. "A square is identical to a circle" is a ready example. It amounts to talk about a square circle, a figure that is an impossibility. The figures of themselves in the statement possess properties precluding any compatibility, any co-existence. The mind perceives this incompatibility of properties, this impossibility of conjunction among them, enabling it to declare the statement to be about something that is impossible.

The terms 'man' and 'immortality' possess no such incompatibility. There is nothing in either term which would make them mutually exclusive, which would preclude one of the other. In examining both terms, looking at them closely for the information they convey about themselves, we find no conflict suggesting immortality and man to be contradictory of one another, to be impossible one of the other. In searching, then, for evidence about human immortality we will be trying to show how the two terms, man and immortality can be stated of one another, can be conjoined reasonably in a judgment arguing human immortality.

To show that a statement is probable requires amassing a weight of evidence permitting us to reduce the doubt we have regarding what it is we seek to claim. "There are ten planets in the solar system" is a statement about a state of affairs which is not intrinsically impossible, but which we can doubt because we lack evidence for it. If we amass evidence, however, for it, our doubt about it decreases. At some point in the process of discovery we reach a state where the evidence makes the doubt less defensible, but still leaves us short of certainty. Discoveries continue to the point where the fact of a tenth planet becomes likely, though not yet a certainty. The greater the evidence, the more improbable becomes the opposite of that which we have postulated. Actually finding a tenth planet gives us the certainty in our claim because denying the claim is to contradict the facts.

In investigating the hypothesis of human immortality, the certainty in our example of finding the tenth planet has to come by way of a different route, if at all. We came to certainty, indubitability, about a tenth planet because the evidence to make it indubitable was found, i.e., a tenth planet. Our sense faculties, with the aid of various instruments, presented it as an actual act. We did not have to reason to it.

If there is evidence—proofgiving, truth-generating data—for human immortality, it is obvious it is not an object of sense-judgment, of sense-perception. What degree of certainty, then, is possible in assessing the hypothesis?

Not all certainty comes by way of physical evidence. There is certainty we have when we know an assertion to involve a contradiction as, e.g., the assertion "all assertions are false." Our certainty is that this cannot be true; but there is no physical evidence providing that certainty. Its source in this instance is the contradictoriness of a proposition. Certainty about my own existence seems assured by this criterion of contradictoriness too, not by sense-evidence. Denying that I exist seems to involve a contradiction, since for me to deny it surely I must exist. No sense-datum, however, grounds our reasoning this way.

And there are certainties we come to through the process of reasoning in which certain and true premises yield certain and true conclusions. And this certainty in conclusions is possible without the actual testimony of the senses. For example, you know that in an eclipse of the sun the moon comes between the earth and the sun, darkening a part of the earth. If this happened on 12 October 1841 in the area of Europe, you have certainty a century-and-a-half later that a part of Europe was darkened that day, even though you were not there, did not personally have actual sense testimony for the certainty. That is a conclusion powered by premisses that are undeniable. (A solar eclipse darkens part of the earth; On 12 October 1841 there was a solar eclipse with the moon in the path of light to Europe; Therefore, on 12 October part of Europe was darkened, while the rest of it remained unaffected.) To deny the conclusion is to deny the action of an eclipse. It is to deny all the evidence that preceded the conclusion which since it is evidence, you know to be incontrovertible.

In reasoning about immortality we would want to be able to reason similarly, to conclude from the evidence a fact that is not immediately evident. As in the case of the eclipse example, we are seeking a certainty for which the evidence, i.e., the actual encounter with immortality, is not directly present. In the eclipse syllogism my conclusion is as certain as if the evidence were directly before me. To argue similarly for immortality we want a conclusion of the same quality. We want premisses of an argument which, when established as true, generate a conclusion equally true and certain in virtue of those premisses. The conclusion would have the same certainty as if the evidence for immortality were directly before me.

Does any aspect of human existence provide for this force of evidence? That is the subject matter for the subsequent chapters of this book. The evidence set forth we can briefly outline here; e.g., examining man's activity of concept formation. To form general concepts, I suggest, is to exhibit an immaterial capacity. Whatever is immaterial is indestructible. But man forms general concepts.

The strength of the argument will derive from the claim made in each premiss. Importantly, in developing this argument it is on the major premiss, "Whatever is immaterial is indestructible," that the claim for immortality hinges. If destructibility requires separability of magnitudes in what is undergoing the destruction, and it is only material magnitudes that can be so separated, existence without such magnitudes would be free from destructibility.[6]

That is the precise language for the argument. Equally, the argument is: parts are limited material magnitudes—pieces of matter.[7] Whenever something corrupts, it does so by the division of its matter into magnitudes, parts, that the division has separated from each other. A block cut in two is no longer the original block. Cut into a thousand pieces, it is no longer a block. Corruption of material existents takes place only through this separation of parts from the original whole. If corruption occurs only through such parts, what is without them could not corrupt.

In line with our requirements for certainty, asserting immortality as a human characteristic necessitates that we show how we come to assert that whatever is immaterial is indestructible. What certainty can we bring to that claim?

Equally necessary is to establish that man forms general concepts, so that it can be argued convincingly that he exhibits an immaterial capacity. If whatever is material is singular, but man exhibits a power that is not something singular—which he does in his activity of concept formation—then man possesses an immaterial capacity. Thus the proof reads: Whatever is immaterial is indestructible; Some activity of man is immaterial; Some activity of man is indestructible.

This is one way to discourse about human immortality, which we will elaborate in the second chapter. The procedure will be in accord with the requirements of evidence to which we have subscribed. Our reasoning process working towards a conclusion must not, of course, assume the truth of any statement that first needs to be proven. In establishing the existence of concepts, mental representations that are general in nature, then, we will be starting with a datum most familiar to every individual—his activity of conceptualization. That activity will be compared to material existents to determine if there is evidence of difference between the two. That act of comparison is a valid procedure for acquiring evidence of difference since it is only by comparison that differences among things become known.

Our assertion that we do form concepts of things will be based on first pointing out how they are general. That will involve noting the features of our concepts that give them this character of generality. Those features will be the evidentiary grounds for distinguishing the being of concepts from that of material existents. The evidence for our characterization of material existents comes from our direct contact with them, verifiable by an appeal to observation.

Important to the procedure of evidence is to review any argument opposed to a position, since evidence may be acquired in that review. Further establishing that man does exercise a capacity for forming general concepts will proceed by showing that the rejection of generality in concepts implicitly accepts that generality. The argument advanced to explain away our belief in the generality of human conceptualization is itself an argument for that generality. Showing that will strengthen the evidentiary case for the existence of general concepts, and, with it, the immaterial status of man.

The activity of long-term memory in man is a separate area of possible evidence to pursue in chapter three. There we will come to a conclusion by suggesting what the memory's non-localizability in the brain indicates about man: the physical brain and personhood are not the same. Some feature of man, indispensably ingredient to his being the person he is, is not reducible to the tissue that decays at death. If we can establish that irreducibility, we have grounds for suggesting that the death of the brain need not entail the death of the person.

Our conclusion here will not directly establish man's immortality. That is in contrast to the argument from concept formation. Directly establishing human immortality, the object of that argument, will hinge on the certainty we adduce for the claim that corruption occurs only in the presence of material magnitudes, i.e., parts—which are found only in material existents, and that human thought attains to an existence that is other than singular. In the case of long-term memory the method has been one of excluding possibilities that it is materially reducible. That method begins with the brain tissue at large and, successively to the molecular level, rules out the materialist candidates for a material preservation of our awareness of the past. Excluding possibilities, however, does not establish the truth of the contrary since it is always conceivable that some possibility is overlooked, though in this case strongly improbable. This differs from examining the nature of a mental entity, say the *concept,* in that we do not reach the nature of an entity by excluding possibilities as to what it is not. The argument from memory will, as a defense of the immortality thesis, show the improbability of its materiality—an improbability that reasoning about the neurological data powerfully grounds. It will strengthen the thesis that the brain is not the storehouse, the *locus of* those memories that so much make what the individual person, his sense of identity, is. An important identifying feature of each personality, the data indicate, is not confined to place; it is non-spatial.

That suggests that human personality transcends a limit we have always associated with life, i.e., spatiality. It suggests a feature of man not constrained by this life, this order of space-time. We have already seen, however, that it was precisely the restriction of human existence to this life of space-time that was an *assumption*

that could not be proven. And because it could not be proven, re-
stricting everything human to this life—one argument that has
been used to deny immortality—was unwarranted. The fact of
long-term memory in man shows how unwarranted that assumption is.

The structure of human awareness—the evidence it provides
for human immortality—is the next field, chapter four, for
gathering certainties about it. If awareness can be shown in its
structure to differ from the physical world, we have identified
another way in which man differs from things physical. In his
most immediate commerce with the world, the way of that
commerce suggest a non-physical activity of human existence.
Like concept formation, which prehends the world through gen-
eralities only after repeated experiences with the world, human
consciousness also argues for a non-material feature of man: but
in this case in each and every individual experience man has of
the world. The way it differs from physicality is different from the
way in which the concept does. This difference, that is, its
structure as other than the physical, expands the case for
doubting the identity of the person with the physical, with his
body, of personhood with the biological. What happens to the
one is not all that happens to the other.

In this regard it will be important to show how assumptive is
the materialist belief that human awareness is a product of neuro-
bodily functions, of a tissue mass called the brain. The more
dubious that view, the more dubious its concommitant that the
end of bodily brain function is the end of awareness capability. A
way to suggest that consciousness is not a bodily product is to
show what difficulties one encounters when assuming that it is.
That would further erode the identification of personhood with
the physical, the destructible.

Our argument, accordingly, will be to show that if the materialist account of consciousness were correct, consciousness could
not take place. As with the discussion of long-term memory, our
method will be to examine at length the neurophysiology/chem-
istry of the human brain. So examined, the impossibility of the
materialist account of consciousness should become clear.

This will be no minor exercise. Its merit lies in taking the materialist account of consciousness on its own terms and seeing
what results from that account. Granting an opponent's premisses
and seeing where they lead is the surest footing for conducting

serious search into the argument he offers. Attentiveness to the demands of evidence requires such a setting. We therefore seek to identify what does or does not qualify as evidence for truth claims. Given a statement one claims to be true we must consider what the claimant offers as his evidence. If what he offers turns out either to invalidate or to make impossible what he is claiming, then what he has adduced for his position cannot be evidence.

We will argue that this is the situation with materialism. What it has presented as evidence for its claim equating bodily death with personal extinction is not evidence. Not evidence because what it has offered as evidence would make impossible the very existence of that for which it claims it is offering the evidence. To wit, to argue that consciousness is merely a bodily process, a neural event, is to make consciousness impossible.

The nature of our evidence in this case, then, is to give certainty that materialist explanations of consciousness's origins do not possess the certainty they claim; nor, thus, the assertions deriving from those explanations. Among them is "man is mortal."

Consciousness in its structure presents itself as being *of* things, whereas nothing physical so presents itself. Our language bears out this recognition. We speak of consciousness as being *of* a tree, *of* a house, *of* a lawn. We never attribute this feature "of to things physical." Our most unreflective mode of speech, points to our understanding that consciousness and the physical world do differ.

That they do differ in their structure, as even common speech seems to recognize, has a weight of evidence that the materialist account of consciousness fails to provide. Only a materialist hypothesis completely different from the current could present a difficulty to the thesis of consciousness' difference from physical existence. To the extent that it is implausible such a hypothesis could arise and be sustained can we measure the cogency of claiming this difference. What we argue in chapter four is that no neurophysiological occurrence resulting from sensory stimuli can be the act of consciousness, or productive of it. Only a materialist hypothesis that exclude sensory stimuli as essential to human consciousness could be a challenge to that thesis. To so exclude sensory stimuli appears totally unsustainable, thus leaving in place the claim that consciousness is not reducible to the brain, for the brain is physical. Consciousness, then, is indestructible, assuming that only physical existence is destructible.

The structure of our argument in this case, then, will have syllogistic premises similar to those in our discussion of concept formation. In the latter our premises are, Man is immaterial; The immaterial is indestructible; Therefore man is indestructible. That man is immaterial the evidence from his possession of general concepts shows. Evidence for the indestructibility of the immaterial requires that only what is material, what has parts separable from parts by which it is composed, be destructible. If destruction of an existent can occur only through such composition by parts, then only material existence is destructible.[8] The force of our certainty hinges on the end to an individual existent occurring no other way. Since we have no evidence that it does, the claim of immaterial existence being indestructible possesses virtual certainty.

In the case of consciousness, our premises are: Consciousness is immaterial; The immaterial is indestructible; Therefore, consciousness is. Here it is the impossibility of the current materialist account of consciousness being true that is the basis for the first premise. Any other materialist hypothesis, it should become clear in chapter four, would have to exclude sensory stimuli in its explanation of how consciousness occurs. If this is shown, consciousness' immateriality would then appear evident. Our basis for the first premise has the force of evidence if, in a materialist hypothesis, sensory stimuli in any way must have causative interaction with neurological tissue for consciousness to occur. A materialist hypothesis not claiming this interaction appears virtually inconceivable. That inconceivability has the appropriate rigor by which the evidentiary quality of the statement "Consciousness is immaterial" ought to be judged.

What possibilities of evidence, finally, are available in the near death, out-of-body experience (ODE) discussed so widely today? How are we to reason about the testimony of its claimants? The veridicality of their claims—the fact that what they claim to have witnessed in their comatose out-of-body state can be verified by bodily-conscious witnesses as actually having happened—is an area meriting detached scrutiny. What doubts do the claims of the near-death ODE raise, and how fantastic are they? To what criteria should we hold those claims, and to what criteria their critics? How plausible is the explanation by critics for the veridicality of the ODE? How can a human being whose bodily sense capacities have ceased functioning relate information, upon recovery, about his earthly surroundings learned in his ODE if the sense-faculties are his only route to knowledge of the world? If sensation is bodily, but the insensate in their ODE have awareness of the world, is it that awareness does not require the body?

Consequently, the evidence gathered from academics and physicians on the near-death ODE and its veridicality comprise chapter five. The implications for the immaterialist assertion unfold as the conditions for that veridicality are made clear. Can they be biological? How can they, if the senses, inoperant in the near-death ODE, are bodily? That raises additional doubt on the identification of human existence with the corporeal, an identification that has been the basis for denying immortality.

The point, then, is made. Certainty requires evidence, either from the terms themselves of a proposition claimed to be certain, or from evidence the denial of which would be a contradiction of what is the case. The former is in no need of proof It is self-verifying, as in the claim "No effect is without a cause." In the latter, a claim requires evidence to be accepted as true. On its own, the claim, without evidence seen as its backing, is dubious. To establish its truth evidence is brought to bear which, when viewed all together, when viewed in its totality, forces the mind to a conclusion that what the evidence certifies is not otherwise. In this way too the mind reaches certainty. The state of certainty is reached when data before the mind disallow a judgment other than that to which the data have led it. The state of truth is reached when those data presented to the mind are truth-giving. Truth-giving certainty is the criterion we have set for judging the arguments in the immortality debate.

In forming a proof for the indestructibility of human person-hood—in attempting to establish that as a certainty—we know that if matter is destructible, we must look for evidence of what is not matter as a first step in identifying an existence that may subsequently show itself to be indestructible. And if it is man who is to be indestructible, we must look for a feature in him that is not material. From the immensity of existence we are rapidly able to eliminate almost everything in it from what must be inspected in our search for immaterial existence. Once the question of the possibility of immortal being is broached, we find the field of inquiry immediately narrowed. We are able to focus almost at once on that which must be appraised for evidence of immateriality. This attention to the conduct of evidence then frames the issue in terms commensurate with what is to be set forth: If all that is immaterial is indestructible, and a feature of man is immaterial, in some way man must be indestructible.

Thus sketched is the route of evidence. The subject of inquiry has presented the route to be taken, has pointed to what it is necessary to establish if an answer is to be reached. It has given us certainty as to how we must proceed. The subject of inquiry itself, then, is a sort of evidence inasmuch as it is evidence that breeds certainty.

In assessing evidence for human immortality, showing what does not constitute evidence against it completes the route of evidence. This further use of the criterion of certainty and evidence clears the path so that it can be trod more surely in moving to establish immortal being. Adherence to this criterion of evidence and certainty is what has prompted the discussion along the lines it has taken here. That adherence establishes immortal being as defensibly warranted by the premises brought to bear in our discussion on the indestructibility of non-material existence. Further elaborated, the ensuing chapters will attempt to show as virtually untenable the materialist hypothesis that at death man is simply destroyed.

NOTES

1. To deny that coming to rest, to an end, in inquiry indicates knowledge with regard to that which provoked the inquiry is, arguably, self-contradictory. it appears to admit what it is denying, since to deny something (and claim *eo ipso* that that denial gives knowledge) is itself a coming to rest. This is clear if the denial is by way of argument, for an argument presumably at some point comes to an end. If the denial is simply one for which no argument is advanced, that denial is still a coming to rest for the mind in that with the denial the claim it is making presumably settles, brings to an end, the issue for the one who is making the denial. Additionally, to advance evidence for the denial's validity is likewise self-defeating, for it is evidence that brings inquiry to an end.

2. There are different "spaces," as physics makes well-enough known. The space of human experience is Euclidean space. I use Euclidean geometry here not as a geometry that is universally true for all "spaces," but only to select an example about a certainty that is easily accessible to every human experience.

3. The unalterability applies so far as the three-dimensionality of space, to which the geometry of common spatial experience applies, remains unaltered.

4. The syllogism is a procedure of reasoning that argues for a claim by means of statements known as premises. The common form has two premises, known as a major and a minor, which when conjoined in thought yield a third, the conclusion. In a correct syllogism the conclusion is immediately traceable to and derivable from the major and minor premiss. The following is an example: (Major) A is B; (Minor) B is C; (Conclusion): Therefore, A is C. By itself, without the work and presence of the major and minor premiss, "A is C" can be doubted. If, i.e., the statement "A is C" were made to me without sating the major and minor premiss that make it true, I could question its veracity. once, however, I

heard the reasoning behind the statement, which the major and minor premiss as true provide, I can no longer doubt its veracity. When seen as a conclusion from premises that are themselves true, the statement "A is C" is itself prehended as true.

5. Directly, in that the difference is not arrived at through a process of reasoning but rather by a non-inferential comparison of living existents with non-living.

6. By material existent I mean what is commonly meant—a three dimensional solid. This immediately rules out any conception of matter as an energy field of sorts, with varying degrees of compression. That view seems to be the position of quantum mechanics: matter is a certain energy-wave frequency with no difference in kind, then, from energy. Energy has no surface, however, while we quite clearly are aware of beings with surface. It is these such beings that are meant by the term "material existents," which are composed ultimately of inert bits whose conjunction is responsible for our awareness of surface in the beings present to sense-perception. It is the diremption of this conjunction, the severance of the unity of, cohesion among, these constituent bits that is material decay, destruction of the material object.

7. While space is a magnitude, its partibility is not as identifiable as the presence of parts in other existents. One reason for this is that space is not an actually existent individual, one thing among, next to, others. We do not see space corrupting because there is only one space. And that space we conceptualize as the limitless extent for receiving all bodies. What we do see is different bodies in a relation of separateness to one another. That indicates space may be differently occupied depending on the body occupying it. This differentiability of occupation gives us the basis for speaking of parts to space: if space had no parts, then whatever occupied it, it would appear, would have to occupy all of it, and thus be one. Accordingly, space has a corruptibility about it inasmuch as it is into parts that corruption occurs. Its determinability by bodies suggests a partness about it that incorruptible existents do not have.

8. The ultimate constituents of our universe are material,, i.e., corruptible, because of their divisibility. They must, that is, have parts because, however infinitesimal those constituents, they must be extended. Were they not extended they would be mathematical points—entities that have no extension. Since they have no extension, no sum of them—however large—could. Everything we experience in the world has extension, however. The ultimate bits comprising the universe and things in it must be extended, therefore, and thus possessed of parts. That these parts are not infinite in number is evident from the fact that an infinite number of parts could never be completed. There are, then, ultimate components to the objects of our world which, because of their extensibility, we know, must be corruptible. That is the same as calling them material.

II
The Argument
from Concept Formation

A question arises in the mind whenever that about which we raise the question presents itself as not completely grasped, not fully known. Inquisitiveness arises only from an absence of evidence regarding that about which we inquire. In the case of immortality, how did the notion itself, about whose veracity we are inquiring, first arise? There are no sense-data that correspond to it, making suspect any theory of knowledge that restricts human thought to such data.

Might not the origins of the notion be found in our ability, however coarsened, to think of something as being "without end"? The closest we come, in the case of immortality, to representing such thought to ourselves is the image of recurrence—life returning again and again. Despite our inability to picture deathlessness to ourselves in any other way than through this sense-image of bodily reanimation, we know that our thought of immortality is more than this. For example, we may be thinking of liberation from physical constraints. Recurrence of life is not a useful image in such a case. Yet the term 'immortality' does have an objective referent in which nonphysical constraint is a meaningful reality. Thus, the image of our bodies in a garden rich with delights without end is not a productive way to convey the thought of immortality either. Physical constraints, which we always associate with our bodies, conveys with it the idea of a limitation that is incompatible with the idea of existence without end.

That we can in fact think in terms of something "without end" is an important point to make in asking how this notion of immortality arose. Given our capacity so to think, one need not claim that the idea arose from some religious declaration in the far-distant past. (The very antiquity of such a declaration would, for some, be sufficient reason to hold it in derision.) Nor need one suggest that the idea came from dreams our ancestors had about the dead, in which dreams, as it were, the dead appeared— as they do even in our own dream images—a suggestion giving the idea a phantasmagoric origin. A more pedestrian explanation—and, for that reason, probably more tenable—can be found in the ability each individual has of thinking any wished-for object as without end. However the idea arose, the explanation of its origin will not gain us access to endless existence. The test is whether such ways of thinking have legitimacy in the case of how we conceptualize human existence.

Unlike our awareness of the world, in which objects are prehended directly, i.e., are immediately evident, no such evidence for a direct acquaintance with immortality exists. Through my sense-faculties I have a direct, non-mediated, acquaintance with this desk. I do not reason to its existence. There are no premises that will lead me to the assertion that it exists. it is just there, and my doubting that it might or might not be, does nothing to that fact. is,

In the question of immortality, the evidence that we must look for is that which points to a feature in man that is incorruptible. If death is bodily corruption, and corruption is our surest sign that burial may take place, might there be in the person now dead an element that does not corrupt? It would have to be an element totally ingredient, intrinsic, to his life and activity as the human being he is for incorruptibility to have any personal significance. It would have to be a capacity that made him human, the very being that he is, such that without it he could not, and would not, be the being he is.

If there were such an element, then the being he is would not cease with bodily decomposition. His very being would be constitutively incorruptible.

The ground for deliberating such a constitutively incorruptible dimension in man has philosophic furrows. And they are deep. Concentrated attentiveness to that reasoning, the work of this chapter is merited since it does not lend itself to a cursory once-over. One would not think reasoning about immortal existence would.

It is to the medieval thinker Thomas Aquinas that the argument for this chapter first turns. In developing those lines of thought he presented for the immortality thesis a present-day treatment of the subject will go quite far. Examining that activity which confirmed for Aquinas an immaterial power in man and therefore human immortality may make that a credible claim.[1]

That activity in man, for Aquinas, is human intellection. Specifically, the mind's power to conceive properties that are the same in things which are in all other respects different offers him evidence about that which we can reason to personal survival, immortal personhood. The mind's apprehension of realities formed through its interaction with sense-objects it judges in some way to be the same evidences for him that immateriality.

The argument is that the concepts we form have a feature that material existents do not, namely, generality. When a property is found to be common to a number of such existents, the mind forms a concept of that property. Through that concept it knows those existents to be in some way the same despite any other differences they may have. It is in this that the generality of the concept arises—in its being that cognitional content by which objects otherwise different are known to be the same.

This generality is found in no material existent. Each object of the sense-world, from which the concepts in question are drawn, is singular, individuated by matter. To form these concepts, then, requires a power that is not material. Therefore man has an immaterial power.

All sense-objects are material. Their spatio-temporal determinations—the physical properties of a thing—make that plain. And all sense-acquaintance is with material things, which are always given as singular—given their spatio-temporal conditions; but not all awareness is of what is only singular.

If that is true, not all human activity, Aquinas is saying, is material. If a mental content shows features that no material thing does, then not all human awareness is material.

The process productive of that awareness likewise could not be. The reason is this: Once you establish that not all existence, as in the case of the concept, is material, then you may divide existence into being either material or immaterial. There is no middle—ground, no third category, of which existence admits. And materiality and immateriality are mutually exclusive: neither can be in the other. An immaterial process or activity, therefore, could not be the effect of a material power. Otherwise, it would be coming from nothing. Since something cannot come from nothing, only an immaterial power could cause what is immaterial. Immaterial activity cannot be the work of material being. Its degree of perfection (as evident, for example, in its absence of physical constraints), exceeds that of matter. Plainly, then, given the rather uncomplicated truth that something cannot come from nothing, material being cannot produce immaterial being. And Aquinas holds that the concepts we form are immaterial.

In certain intellection the mental content is clearly not of a singular thing. Rather, in being of features, properties, that are the same in different things it is of features that are general in range as opposed to singular. That is, it is of features that are common to things in a way no singular thing can be to another. If so, the mind transcends singular, and thus material, existence. For material existence is always singular.

Human thought penetrates to characteristics of things in respect of which those things, despite individuating differences, are known to be the same. In its conceptualization of that sameness lies the mind's power of generality. The concept's generality lies in the indifference of its applicability to those beings so conceptualized. The cognitional content is genuinely general because the feature (or set of features) of which it is is not confined to a single existent, but is instead of a feature (or set) existing throughout a number of existents. In penetrating to that feature (or set) the mind is given a content of things by means of which it can classify those things by the concept it so forms. In that act of classification through the concept lies the mind's activity of generalization.

Nothing singular, however, can give the concept its generality. That generality of content lies in the commonality of features, characteristics, among singular existents differing in every way except for those features, characteristics, which they exhibit in common. But of its very being the singular existent cannot be common to other material existents: it is incommunicable. In the mind's prehension through the concept, then, of those features things exhibit in common it has exercised an activity entirely other than singular existence. It has exercised, accordingly, an immaterial act. Two examples will give detail to that claim.

(1) Take the notion 'triangle'. I can think triangle indifferently as to its particular configurations, e.g., scalene, isoceles, equilateral. Each is different in shape, each unlike the other. Their differences, though, do not limit the mind from thinking

triangle correctly of each of them. Through a number of contacts with the figures and subsequent comparison among them the mind locates a property in common to, equal throughout, them, a feature not limited to, exhausted by, any one of them. That feature these figures reveal to the mind as their basic, irreducible constituent. Without it they would cease to be what they are, triangles.

It is this conceptualization of *triangle* that interests us here. We conceive the property triangle as common to different material things, a conceptualizability for which no material existent can account. Each material existent is singular, i.e., not repeated in any other. Features in it, however, are; and the concept is of those features. No material existent is common to a number of different material existents. But the concept, in this case *triangle*, is. Nor is there any material existent that has about it the trait "common to many things." In no sense-reception is the trait "common to many things" given. It is not a sense- feature; none of the five senses conveys it. The concept, however, as in the case *triangle*, does. It has a note about it not accessible through sense-acquaintance, to which only the singular existent is present, a note through which the mind conceives an attribute, *triangle*, as the same in things otherwise different.

From no material existent, then, could the general concept so arise. The concept's presence in the mind, accordingly, would evidence a capacity in the mind that is not material. If commonality is not derivable from, locatable in, material existence but nevertheless exists in the mind, clearly something about the mind is not material.

This generality of mental content that Aquinas so compressedly advanced, a generality immortalists cite as evidence for existence unending, was denied by the eighteenth-century empiricists. Their denial came by arguing that no sensuous representation[2] is general in nature, but always particular, always singular.

That in fact is true. And no one would dispute them on it. But a concept is not a sensuous representation. And it is the *concept* that philosophers asserting immortality argued was general in scope.

It is Berkeley who is credited with the empiricist view.

For myself I find indeed I have a faculty of imagining or representing to myself the ideas of those particular things I have perceived and of

variously compounding and dividing them. . . . the idea of man that I
frame to myself must be either of a white or a black, or a tawny, a
straight. or a crooked, a tall, or a low, or a middle-sized man. I cannot
by any effort of thought conceive the abstract idea above described.[3]

Since my mental representation formed of man is always of a particular individual, the generality or universality attributed to our
idea of man must be, for Berkeley, in error.

When I think of *man,* however, to correct Berkeley, I think of
a rational, living, sentient, corporeal being. And that term 'man'
broadly applies over all such beings that fit the description. From
there the generality emerges. In forming a concept applicable to
all men the mind disregards individuating differences such as
height, shape, color, and proceeds to those features in which individuals agree. Going beyond the differences of each individual
that sensation gives us, e.g., the differences in voice, color, height,
it notes that some beings possess a body, assimilate food and grow,
exhibit sensation and rationality. In all such attributes they agree,
irrespective of all individuating differences. Individualizing
features have been left aside, and only what is common to these
beings—is the same throughout them—has been retained.
Conjoined, these notes fund the concept 'man', whose generality
lies in its applicability to all those beings wherein such notes are
conjoined.

Were my idea of man of a particular individual, say Michael
Jordan, the basketball player, I could not apply it indifferently to
others. For no one else is Michael Jordan. To account for this indifference of applicability, the empiricists held that it was by
convention or custom that we came so to apply the term. This
position, though, tacitly admits what it purports to deny, namely,
the general nature of certain concepts. Showing this should
advance the philosophic claim for immortality.

How does one know when the convention applies? To differentiate it from the unconventional, convention requires a
criterion for its applicability. And a criterion is uniform throughout the instances in which it is invoked or used. Thus the
empiricists are in fact acknowledging what they claim to be
denying, to wit: the general nature of our concepts. In citing convention as the grounds for our general terms, they are
acknowledging a sameness throughout different instances. That
acknowledgment, that recognition, of a content that is uniform
throughout different things is precisely what a general concept is,

however. That is what permits things otherwise different to be classified—known by one term. To admit convention, then, as the grounds for our use of general terms is to admit that some ideas are actually general in their being.

This necessity for a uniformity of content between the criterion and different sense-particulars is granted in the empiricists' own argument. The criterion by which we agree to call sense-particulars by the term 'man', e.g., could not be totally unlike the sense-particulars so called. Assume it was, that it remains the same, uniform throughout, but the sense-particular in each case is wholly different from it. How could the criterion apply uniformly, which is what convention requires, to these different sense-particulars if between it and the sense-particulars in question there was nothing uniform? It couldn't; the uniformity necessary—implied in the very notion of a criterion's applicability—is absent. To cite convention, then, as the grounds for our use of general terms is to admit that our ideas do in fact exhibit a generality of content, that we have general concepts. For the recognition of a content that is uniform through things otherwise different is exactly what a general concept is.

David Hume, perhaps a more trenchant thinker than Berkeley, phrased the empiricist denial of general concepts a bit more subtly. It was through habit, he held, that we came to use an identical label, one word, for objects. It was through the process of repeatedly using the same name for objects that we became accustomed to applying the class name. There was no concept as such behind the name, merely, it seems, something akin to an involuntary association of mental states in and among each member of a society using a so-called class name among themselves.[4]

Habits, however, to answer Hume, are reactions, ways of doing things arising from circumstances that are known to possess traits in common. One would think Hume knew this. Becoming accustomed, to habituate oneself, to one word over another is to imply a selection/discrimination process originally by which the word or utterance in question came to be used for the property that it is. Selection, however, requires a standard by which whatever is selected is so in the different instances that it is. And that is to admit to the recognition of sameness throughout things otherwise different—which recognition is precisely what is meant by the concept.

To put it another way: in a language's earliest stages an utterance is agreed upon, selected, that will convey "X" to the hearer rather than "Y." As the population using that language increased, its members became accustomed to vocalizing that utterance which was originally selected whenever "X" appeared. This much is true.

One does not, however, through the process of becoming accustomed, come to recognize that different objects are "X." We do not agree among ourselves that we will select "X" among the objects of our experience and then become accustomed to "X." We recognize a sameness in objects which, though they differ in every other way can be called the same in virtue of "X." And through that recognition the utterance that was originally agreed upon to mean, indicate, "X" is made. The basis for our utterance then is the cognitional content of sameness ranging over different things—in other words, the concept. Hume's theory of habit, in that it requires this recognition of sameness in different things, is an admission to the presence of the concept.

The basis for classification of objects, then, is not, as the empiricists held, outside the actual interaction of the mind with its object. The concept is not a social artifice, a linguistic device of grammarians, introduced from without to facilitate communication among the members of a society. The empiricist argument in implicitly admitting what it was claiming to disprove, namely, the real generality of mental content, makes that plain enough. Hume's argument that class names are strictly habits that we form is itself acknowledgment of this sameness of feature or circumstance in different situations. It was a puzzling, if not disingenuous, attempt to avert a conclusion that the hypothesis of habit actually requires. The basis for our recognition of sameness in things otherwise dissimilar, which is to say the foundation for the general nature of our concepts, is not outside those objects whence our concepts are drawn. The grounds for classification must be in the objects themselves. For it is these that we classify.

It cannot be, though, their individuating differences that account for their selection for classification. In such a case, we would be back in, those circumstances just shown to be impossible. What accounts for the indifference of applicability in our general terms is the entitative content of those sense-objects, that content the mind finds repeated throughout those objects. It is by that repetition of content that those sense-objects, divested by the mind of their individuating differences, are classed under one heading. It is this content which ground the class notion so formed as a universal concept in the mind as genuinely general. This content, in providing for sameness of feature in things otherwise different, is prehended by the mind as common to those things. In this prehension lies the generality of conception. In whatever future case the mind comes across the sameness of feature in a material existent, it will conceptualize it by that sameness of feature as belonging to a class of things, in which conceptualization, accordingly, resides the evidence for the general nature of man's ideas.

(2) Additionally, take the example of the term 'animal'. We recognize features, properties, that are the same in many things which otherwise differ. In a causal theory of knowledge it is those things that furnish the mind the data by which it grasps that property which is the same in those things. Through comparison of remembered and present acquaintance with such things that property becomes stabilized in the mind as a concept. The world is fashioned such that things, because of their sameness, arrange themselves in classes. And the concept is the mental content of that class.

The sameness, because it can be prehended through a graded scale of different beings, as in the case of the attribute "animal," offers considerable reliability to the assertion of the mind's immaterial status. The concept "animal" differs sharply from material, from singular, existence in a quite evident way. No material existent possesses the notes "dog," "cow," "eagle," "shark," "ant," "snail," and "man." To do so, the existent would have to be all those notes at once. I can think of a material existent possessing any one of these characteristics, but not of a material existent possessing all of them, because it cannot. No individual thing can have the traits that make both a bluefish and a lion. My concept animal has no such restriction. Within it are the traits of all movent living things.

So analyzed, the concept is patently non-material. It differs from all material existents. Possessed of such conceptualization, man himself must likewise differ. In forming class notions— concepts of entitative sameness in numerically different material existents—man goes beyond singular, beyond material, existence to what is general in its nature. We already noted the identity of material existence with singular existence. Each existent in our sense-acquaintance is spatio-temporally determined, by which it is individuated, singularized. Those spatio-temporal determinations are the material properties of size and volume, with temporality being fixed by the mass and solidity of those spatial dimensions. The duration, the temporal span, of a physical existent is inextricably linked to its resistance to outside factors. The object's solidity is that resistance. Everything encountered in sense-experience is spatio-temporal, and the material existent, as always spatio-temporal, is singular. Singularity resides, then, in the spatio-temporal status caused by materiality, which shows itself in no way other than the spatio-temporal determinations encountered in sense-experience.

In forming the class notion the mind goes beyond the singular. The concept's generality, as patently non-material, is an indication, then, of human incorruptibility if material existence alone is subject to corruption. This generality, though, is not the only indication of that possible incorruptibility. In its concept formation, specifically in the example before of "animal," the mind—in so forming the concept—reaches an awareness level that again is non-material. If encountering that level requires a capacity, a power, to so encounter it, the mind has an immaterial capacity. If to form such a concept, with this non-material feature, of genuine entitative constituency in things requires a capacity to so form it, the mind exercises an activity that is not material.

For the mind to be incorruptible, the argument of the immortalists has run, this non-material feature is a necessity. Non-materiality alone is evidence of incorruptible existence. Only material existence, they have argued, is corruptible because it alone has the condition for corruption, that is, constituency by parts. This argument is equally as exacting as that for the non-materiality of human conceptualization. That should be expected when the subject is.

Accordingly, we may reflect that however objects are encountered or interpreted human experience abounds with entities that are multi-composed. Conceivably there is no experience of anything not composed of simpler qualities or constituents, of something that is absolutely simple. The furniture of the world is always present to us, we find, as composite, irrespective of the thing experienced. Under the microscope all things are further analyzable to the power of the microscope: the greater the power, the more building blocks discovered. Even primary colors—those reducible to no other—are not experienced as simple. We do not experience the color red, but a red object. There is no experience of color without relation to figure, two factors. The point is not that we cannot experience something absolutely simple. It is simply that we do not.

In our immediate experience our direct acquaintance is with composed objects. Upon reflection we know that they are composed. The object's composition makes it analyzable to the mind which, in the activity of understanding, always moves to the simpler. Explanation involves simplification. Something is explicable if it permits simplification, if it can be made simpler. Once simplified it is easier for the mind to identify the relation of an object's ingredients to themselves and to the object itself.

Plato's contribution from his *Phaedo*[5] on the nature of the composite and simple is instructive here. From it emerges further precisions on that condition cited to be required for human immortality, namely, immateriality. Man must in some way be immaterial, it has been argued, if any credence can be given to the immortality assertion.

The *Phaedo* tenet is this: whatever is composed, composable, is corruptible. Whatever is divisible can be broken down into simpler parts, i.e., into the parts of which it is composed. Unless an entity be composed of parts, such entity cannot decompose into its parts.

Does this have any relevance to the raw matter that goes to build the galaxies and our world? It does, if it is only the existent composed from it that is corruptible.

It was probably Descartes' Fifth Meditation[6] that most concisely identified what we generally regard to be the nature of this physical stuff, matter—this imporous inertia.[7] Matter is what has parts outside of parts, is located in space, and extended. To be in any way material is to possess at least these three characteristics; and one more, destructibility.

Anything that is material is divisible into parts less complex, or of smaller quantity, if the constituent parts are qualitatively identical. In all cases it is a loss of identity: point B, the state of being broken up, is not identical to point A, the status of not being so broken. The point is plain: materiality, because of its partibility, is dissolubility.

Extension is a notable attribute here. To have parts is to occupy a place and while occupying that place to prevent anything else from that occupation. To have extension is to take up space—put more simply, to be in a place. Whenever a place is taken, it has been so by matter whose occupation is configured precisely to the place taken.

This is a matter of general observation. Inasmuch as a material thing has occupied space it does so through extension. The extent of its occupation is limited, and those extents are called parts. In this regard 'part' has a precise meaning: limited material extension of a larger mass. We often use the term to mean role or power—as in the actor's "part" in the play, or that "part" of man by which he desires. It is in its exact primary dictionary meaning, however, which neither of these usages conveys, that appears here, and which gives the argument the precision called for.

We observe decomposition to occur only materially, and that in only one way, *viz.*, into parts of lesser magnitudes. The decomposing material thing gets smaller, reduces in magnitude—extension—by a reduction of parts, and then, in full decomposition, by their eventual elimination. Once eliminated this space—extension—it took up becomes "empty."

Because decomposition takes place into lesser magnitudes,[8] it would not be unreasonable to hypothesize that in the absence of magnitude, extension, decomposition would not occur. But we have already seen that to be a material thing is at once to be composed of parts because every material thing occupies space. And that occupation implies extension, the fractional extent of which occupation is called a part, a corporeal magnitude.

Is it not, however, only a material thing, the advocates of immortality point out, that is so composed? What magnitudes go to make up the concept "animal," or "dog," or "triangle"? What extension do these concepts have? And what loss of magnitudes do they undergo? Into what lesser magnitudes, if so composed, do these concepts corrupt? Into smaller concepts of "animal," "dog," "triangle"? Or broken up concepts of such? Conversely, are these concepts formed by accretions of magnitudes, one to the other? And how do you divide them? You cannot. The concept is not partible, completely lacking magnitudes whose dimunition is the process of destruction.

And is the concept ever destroyed? If in your mind you ignore the mental note "quadruped" in the concept dog, you have not destroyed the concept "dog." You simply no longer have it. The concept itself remains unaltered. Otherwise, you have the situation in which if I don't think the concept it has no existence. Were that so, no one else would have the concept when I was not thinking it. Not thinking a concept or disregarding one of its constituents does not change or terminate its being. Otherwise, every time we ceased thinking the concept, to reacquaint ourselves with it would require that we repeat the concept-formation process. That means acquiring the concept only after repeated contacts with the individual sense-particulars about which we originally formed the concept. And that reacquaintance process simply does not happen. Nor does it help to say one's concept, e.g., of dog, is destroyed at one's death. That is to assume what has yet to be proven, *viz.*, that death is the extinction of consciousness and mental being.

In the material being, though, take away enough parts and its existence is irretrievable. Material dissolution is accomplished by such diminution. While in restoring the note "quadruped" to the concept dog after having ignored it you resurrect the concept dog in your awareness, in material existence no such restoration returns existence. So far as we know, corruption takes place only in the presence of magnitudes which, because they occupy space, are reducible. Spatiality appears inextricably conjoined to material dissolubility. For magnitudes are spatial, and it is only into lesser magnitudes that corruption occurs. A material thing is a magnitude occupying space such that no other occupation of that space is possible without the elimination of that material thing. If it is only into lesser magnitude—lesser parts—that corruption can occur, what does not admit of such magnitudes would appear incorruptible. Since every material thing admits of such lesser magnitudes, what does not would be immaterial—as well as incorruptible.

This conclusion was inevitable except apparently, to the eighteenth-century thinker, Immanuel Kant. In what is commonly referred to as his reply to Moses Mendelssohn, Kant argued that a being need not have parts to lose its existence. That being could lose its existence through a finely graded diminishment of its existence. We could conceive the loss of existence occurring by degrees, that is, and that would not require the presence of extensive magnitude. Consciousness, Kant points out, e.g., has such degrees of intensity in the absence of physical magnitude. Could not the loss of existence therefore occur by successive diminutions of intensive reality in a being that has no parts? Eventually, according to this argument, successive diminution of its degree of being would render it non-existent.[9]

We have no experience that loss of existence occurs this way. Not even in the case of consciousness; we could not experience the loss of its existence, if ever there were such a loss. Such a loss would be tantamount to the end of personal existence, of which no experience is possible. And it is experience that we have chosen as our standard of judgment, since evidence does not seem to be attainable any other way. That we might think of something occurring, and that it does, are two different realities.

If we think to ourselves this loss of existence by degrees which Kant has in mind, how does this diminishment occur? Since it cannot be by parts, what is it that occurs in each successive decline that eventually ends in the being's non-existence. Does not Kant's statement to Mendelssohn, to have any content at all, require that we conceive of existence as a quality? For it is only quality, experience tells us, that is lost by degrees—as the quality of color on a wall. It is in fact in such terms that Kant's reply speaks, and therefore presumably what he has in mind in his reply. Existence, however, cannot be a quality. Nothing can be a quality of itself, which existence would have to be were it a quality; for quality is always of existence. Kant's model, namely, the degrees of a thing's existence, is inapt. When something exists there are not degrees to its existence. It either exists or it does not. Existing, it does not gain in existence. Existence does not increase in intensity once it occurs, or while it occurs. That should be plain enough. If existence were a quality, however, one would think it should increase in degree if it could decrease by degree. That observation perhaps adds to the inaptness of Kant's model, on which model his argument for the loss of existence in a being without parts depended.

This lethargy in Kant's reply to Mendelssohn makes puzzling its recurrence in Swinburne's 1987 book, *The Evolution of the Soul*.[10] Granting that corruption is by parts, material magnitudes, Swinburne, in a manner reminiscent of Kant, argues that it can also be by the loss of essential properties. And that, he offers, does not entail the breakdown into a being's parts. In probably recognizing that existence cannot be a property, Swinburne chooses as an illustration of his point the liquefication of a metal table. In such a liquefication it would have lost an essential property, hardness, and thus cease to be a table. What makes this example an oddity is that the conversion of metal into a liquid, its liquefication, is possible only by a breakdown of the bonds between molecules or molecular chains, which themselves are material parts of metal.

The facts that experience has made available to us, then, remains intact. It is in materiality that corruption occurs, leaving immateriality incorruptible. The philosophic argument for human incorruptibility, with the objection of its critics reviewed, makes reasonable the claim for human immortality. With each claim in that argument verified by the findings available to human inquiry the syllogistic argument leading to immortality as a reasonable conclusion can be formulated. The strength of that conclusion, we argued in Chapter I, would need the same force of evidence as our eclipse syllogism provided if it were to be at all convincing. The evidence points to grounds for it being so: Whatever is immaterial is incorruptible; Man, because of his activity of concept formation, must be in some way immaterial; Therefore, man in some way must be incorruptible.

NOTES

1. Aquinas's relevant views can be found in his *Summa Theologiae*, I, Q. 85, articles 1, 2, & 3; Q.86, article 1; and *On Being and Essence*, ch. 3, para. 60; *On Truth,*, Q. 10, articles 4, 5.

2. The term is not an oxymoron. To the empiricists states of awareness differ in degree only, not in kind, in—to use Hume's term—vivacity or liveliness (see his *A Treatise of Human Nature*, Book I, Part I, Sec. I). In the empiricists' inventory of human awareness they find no trans-sensate state. All human awareness is for them sense-laden, totally exclusive of non-sensuous content.

The most persuasive reply to the empiricists' denial of genuinely mental states—states of awareness differing in kind from sensate states—is, like them, to perform an inventory of our awareness and ascertain—by using their methodology, that of this inventory of awareness—whether they have missed something. What immediately comes to mind is found in the procedure they used to assert that all human awareness is strictly sensate in kind, to wit, inference itself. There is no object given to any one sense or any combination thereof that transmits a sensation "inference." In using the empiricist methodology of examining all sense-objects from every angle possible I cannot, try as I might, find any sense-object or combination of them that presents the sense-datum "inference," or a faded copy of sense-images that will either. Absent the sense-datum, no sense-faculty or combination of them can furnish an awareness of it. Introspection into the content of the mind's operations is also of no help in locating the origin of this idea called inference for the empiricist. Inference requires memory; the empiricists, however, hold that selfhood, a necessary precondition for memory, is not a sense—datum. They therefore deny it as an object of knowledge. If it cannot be known whether a self exists to perform inference, how can any amount of introspection yield a knowledge of inference? The results of the empiricist methodology would require that we deny it exists, a denial made by means of that very operation their methodology requires they deny exists. That itself should have made the empiricists recognize the error of their claim that all human awareness is sensuous. Apparently, though, it did not.

It is not the case, then, that a full inventory of human awareness yields only sense-representations. In finding "inference" in our inventory of knowledge we are entitled to look for other examples of non-sensuous representations, and ask why the empiricist inventory is incomplete. E.g., we may ask what sensuous image we have of the term 'ignorance'? None, and yet the term is fairly well grasped. Following the rules of study set forth by the empiricists would oblige us to deny any meaning to the term 'ignorance', for no sense-faculty or process of comparison among sense-representations conveys the datum "ignorance." What datum—what sense-impression—, or faded copy of such, do we have of "an absence of knowledge"?

And in the example "triangle," our concept of it is of a figure formed by three lines intersecting by twos in three points and so forming three angles. This concept has patent generality among individual triangles. Our sense-image may be of one that is obtuse-angled, right-angled, or scalene—of something singular. But our concept is not limited to any one of them. It applies to any number of different individual configurations, and this applicability beyond any singular figure differentiates it from the image which, because of its exclusively sensuous content, is particular. The empiricist position is flawed. The awareness of triangle is two-fold. It is not only contained in the sensuous image that the empiricists found. Our awareness of it is also conceptual, which a more scrutinizing inventory of human awareness must include as well.

3. George Berkeley, A Treatise Concerning the Principles of Human Knowledge, 10.

4. David Hume, *A Treatise of Human Nature*, Book I, Part I, Sec. VII.

5. Plato, *Phaedo*, 78b–80c.

6. See René Descartes, *Meditations Concerning First Philosophy*, Fifth Meditation.

7. I am not suggesting Descartes viewed material things the way a so-called realism would; (I take "realism" to be the view of common sense). His characterization of the *res extensa* in the Fifth Meditation does concisely, though, identify those attributes we generally view as basic to matter.

While I do not wish to enter upon the realism versus idealism/rationalism debate about the reality of matter and space, I will make these comments in addition to those made in n. 6, ch. I where I have argued for the distinction between matter and energy-field composition. Here my comments are intended to uphold the objective referentiality of matter as common sense would have it.

Matter's presence is made known directly to me through my awareness of resistance, of an inability to proceed or move any farther without the removal of that resistance. From the sub-atomic level to the level of ordinary experience, matter is just this resistance to move or to be moved. And as resistant, that which resists presents itself to me as other than me inasmuch as I cannot be resistant to myself. Being includes more than me, a world other than me. It includes a non-porous, impassable resistance which we call matter. A material existent that corrupts is the corruption of whatever has that resistance.

And more than resistance points to an external world. The awareness of motion does also. Something moving must be other than me, inasmuch as to be aware of it I must at least not be moving.

I take the non-mental basis of space to be given in my immediate awareness of, direct acquaintance with, my own body and its feelings, sensations. Differing sensations, say pain, are felt in different points in my bodily consciousness. In seeking to attend to them I am immediately aware that they do not coincide. Their simultaneously perceived non-coincidence is the immediate perception of length. Through my tacticle awareness I am immediately, directly, aware of a mass I experience directly to be mine, and through touch perceive these differring pain points as conjoined with that mass. The differing points of pain throughout that mass give me the awareness directly of separation on mass—i.e., of size. The awareness of that separation is the basis for the recognition of distance. Thus, while no sensation has distance or extension, my primitive bodily awareness certifies distance as a genuine datum. In subsequent ventures into the world beyond my body cognate circumstances provide the occasion for judgment to assert the existence of extension or distance. However much that judgment is based on perception, and therefore the extension in question subject to possible mismeasurement, extension's objective existence is not undone. The fact, as discussed above, that my body has size assures me of that. Whenever perception presents to me a mass similar to that in the case of the body, I am entitled to judge of that mass, as I do in the case of the body, an attribute of extension. And if two masses are separate that I perceive, my judgment is not to be faulted for thinking of that separation between them as capable of being filled by another mass—which is tantamount to calling that separation "distance," "extension," or "empty" space.

8. Separation into two equal magnitudes is the destruction of what was, prior to the separation, one. Has there been any loss of matter to the original magnitude if the two new magnitudes both measure equally after the separation? Do two pieces of a 12-inch block equally partitioned measure fully six inches each, i.e., together, fully 12 inches? They cannot, for we can identify the line of partition, which is the evidence of discontinuity between the partitioned parts. It is matter that effects the continuity of the 12-inch block. The pieces divided equally may indeed equal each other. But they do not together equal the mass of the original 12-inch block. Indeed, adding a glue to rejoin the broken parts greatly reduces the evidence of partition because continuity is effected once more (or greatly enhanced) which is the work of matter—in this case the glue. In our example the matter lost in the partitioning would be, for instance, sawdust. Were it restored to the partitioned parts it would, when the parts were rejoined, re-form the continuity of the original 12-inch block since now its full mass has been restored.

9. See Immanuel Kant, *Critique of Pure Reason*, B 413–415. Regarding his distinction between intensive and extensive quantity (magnitude) cf. B 208–10. That Kant equates intensive magnitude with quality I take as following from his claim that sensation has intensive, as opposed to extensive, magnitude. And what is sensation if not a presence of quality to awareness?

10. Richard Swinburne, *The Evolution of the Soul,* (New York: Oxford University Press, 1987), pp. 305–06.

III
The Argument from Memory

That memory exists is self-evident, since to deny it requires that capacity to which the term 'memory' refers. We must remember what it is that we are denying when denying it. Scepticism regarding the existence of a self is shot through with such weaknesses. Memory requires a continuity over time to the one that remembers, and that continuity is selfhood at its minimum. The experience of this continuity, more precisely, is what gives selfhood its human contours. In some regard, memory must also be self-verifying. To doubt memory's veracity requires memory, which it is precisely what we are doubting when the hypothesis is that memory is not self-verifying. For the moment, however, it is the materialist, the reductionist, account of human memory that is our topic. Its claim that memory is totally explicable as a neuro-chemical event, a molecular structure perhaps, or a product of neuronal transmission, is not one that evidence will support. The evidence is lacking that the breakdown of neural structures in bodily decomposition at death is the end of personal memory.

The importance of memory to human individuality, as well as the assertion of that importance, is in little need of explanation. Without memory it is a practical certainty that we could not function in the world. And without memory, an important part of the content of one's uniqueness—the fact that no one else has one's memories—would be non-existent. We would differ from one another little more than robotic figurines.

Memory is the capacity for an event to be mentally present to us for longer than an instant, to take on a permanence that the instant does not give. "Keeping something in mind" and recalling some past event are manifestations of that capacity. Broadly, the presence of this capacity has two opposing explanations. it is a biological process traceable and reducible to neural excitations in the brain; it is not equitable with physical functions at all. If the latter is true, and thus the former false, a constitutive reality in each one of us is not physical. If memory is not corporeal in its being, human reality is not entirely physical; physical death is not the end of one's reality as a human. If the materialist explanation for one component of mind critical to human personality lacks evidentiary backing, it will have to look elsewhere for data to support its claim that mind and the physical brain are the same, that mental states are nothing but physical changes.

It was with the neurosurgical practice of Dr. Wilder Penfield that data came to light in the 1930s about the experimental and clinical inability to specify a place for memory in the brain. The memory that we draw upon in moments of recall and review— long-term memory—as distinguished from the rote memory of habit and repetition is not stored in any part of the brain. It is this, long-term memory, that will focus evidence in this chapter against the reductionist equation of personhood with neural tissue, and the tissue's disintegration with that personhood.

Penfield dealt extensively with correcting epileptic conditions in patients. Before the development of electro-encephalography and electrocorticography, electrical exploration—direct elec- trode stimulation of brain mass—was the neurological procedure to identify the problem site of epilepsy in the brain. Through incision the scalp was drawn back and electrode stimulation begun to pinpoint the epileptic fault site. Once pinpointed, the procedure was surgical excision with the goal of eliminating the cause of epileptic seizure.

> In the course of surgical treatment of patients suffering from temporal lobe seizures . . . we stumbled upon the fact that electrical stimulation of the interpretative areas of the cortex occasionally produces . . . acti- vations of the sequential record of consciousness, a record that had been laid down during the patient's earlier experience. The patient 'relived' all that he had been aware of ill that earlier period . . . as in a . . . 'flashback'.[1]

Electrode stimulation of neural mass brought forth memories in the patient's life involuntarily retrieved through this stimula- tion. The quality of the memories:

> . . . a mother told me she was suddenly aware, as my electrode touched the cortex, of being ill in her kitchen listening to the voice of her little boy who was playing outside in the yard. She was aware of the neigh- borhood noises, such as passing motor cars. that might mean danger to him.

> A young man stated he was sitting at a baseball game in a small town and watching a little boy crawl under the fence to join the audience. Another was in a concert hall listening to music. "An orchestration" he explained. He could hear the different instruments. All these were unimportant events, but recalled with complete detail.[2]

Penfield goes on to present the clinical case of one patient where eighteen points of her brain's right hemisphere were electro-touched in looking for the causal site of her epileptic trauma.

> The succeeding responses from the temporal lobe were 'psychical' instead of sensory or motor. They were activations of the stream of consciousness from the past. . . . (Site 11)—"I think I head a mother calling her little boy somewhere. It seemed to be something that happened years ago." (Site 18a)—"I had a little memory—a scene in a play—they were talking and I could see it—I was just seeing it in my memory."
>   I was more astonished, each time my electrode brought forth such a response. How could it be? This had to do with the mind! I called such a responses "experiential" and waited for more evidence.[3]

Penfield's surprise resulted from what happened with his original intent simply to map out the sensory, the motor, and the speech areas of the human cortex. (1) It was found that cortical responses to electrode cartography—this mapping-out procedure —included recall of past experiences, as in the examples noted. (2) Beyond that, it was found in the surgical excision of known causal sites of epilepsy in the brain's temporal lobes the memories elicited by electrode stimulation of those sites remained intact. The patient still had the memory he reported when the tissue site was first stimulated, but which site was now removed.[4] The site, then, did not contain the memory.[5] Nor could any other area stimulated in further exploration be found to elicit it.

Given the brain's enormous complexity, and thus the chance that the memory originally reported might be located elsewhere, subsequent brain areas of sufficient intricacy were stimulated for purposes of memory excitation—sufficient intricacy so as to be neurologically credible as a site of memory, given memory's own intricacy of composition. In all such cases the memory in question was not found. And those memories elicited in this subsequent electro-exploration were left intact despite tissue mass excision. In cases other than Penfield's report, such as injury to the hippocampus or the mesial thalmus—brain areas shown to be formative in memories—memories formed prior to these injuries were not destroyed. In these traumas, while it is clinically certain that the patient cannot form new memories, his past memories are not extinguished. Brain areas, clinically established as instrumental to the creation of memories, are not in their preservation. The neurological findings, from the method of electro-exploration, is that brain mass does not qualify as the repository of the individual's memory.

The results of this work, reported by Penfield in *The Mystery of the Mind* and with those of Phanor Perot[6], as well as those of Sir John Eccles,[7] and Jacques Barbizet's,[8] was furthered by Michael Marsh in *A Matter of Personal Survival: Life After Death.*[9] Could memory, Marsh asks, be situated in, stored as, a neural groove imprinted by experience—a groove that escaped the excision procedures curative of epilepsy? E. Roy John, Director of New York University's Medical College Brain Research Laboratory, in a 1980 paper, published findings from the research undertaken to confirm or deny the neural-groove hypothesis.

Countless experiments with animals, destroying or removing parts of their brain, as John is cited in the Marsh study, failed to locate the site of any pathway responsible for memory. Additionally, John's paper advanced empirical evidence increasing the hypothesis's implausibility. Brain neurons, John states, often fire spontaneously, e.g., in the absence of any stimulus. They respond unpredictably to any given stimulus, showing no tendency toward sameness of response regardless of the stimulus. They will also respond in the same way to a stimulus relayed by different sense-organs. Given such variability of neuronal activity, neuronal activity in memory could frequently be different. On one occasion it might be a groove formation, another not. The groove hypothesis would then be invalidated. And given science's requirement for predictability, its absence here would disqualify the neural-groove hypothesis as science. Also in support of his rejection of the groove hypothesis John noted that because so many neurons are affected in sense-experience, it is difficult to see how any neural groove could remain unaltered—which it must if it is to be the memory store—from the innumerable neuronal excitations each sense-experience would cause.

Pressing the analysis further, Marsh argues that the fact of a past event's recall after a number of years makes the storage theory of memory unsatisfactory. It is difficult to see how, e.g., in the recollection of an event 40 years past, that recollection is possible without repeated mental reference to it and constant reinforcement. With the brain's neurological structure constantly subject to all kinds of stimuli and chemical processes, the claim that the brain could hold a memory over so many years with no change in content from what is being remembered is not easily credible.[10]

Depth psychiatry, Marsh points out, does note in this regard that many of our long-term memories are retrieved in their original perceptual form. Think of the time your accidentally drank a mixed drink at a summer barbeque when you were a child instead of the lemonade you wanted. The actual percept, though 35 years past, is immediate to mind. Yet my awareness of that past event as past, which my awareness of that event is, rules out, Marsh shows, the memory as some storage trace in the brain. The imagery recall we achieve in long-term memory has no analogue to the notion of trace. "The bear's footprint is his trace," Marsh notes, "but it offers no picture of the bear." In long-term memory, however, the content is pictorial, as in the case of the summer barbeque, redolent with detail.

Nor can the trace hypothesis explain our awareness of past as past. The awareness cannot come from the memory's content, for we have seen from depth psychiatry that it frequently has the perceptuality. the presentness, of the original event. In our bear-footprint analogy, the footprint does not generate an awareness of the trace as trace. Our awareness is of the footprint as the trace of an original. Trace as trace does not contain the original; the original, however, is that which is past. Trace as trace, then, and our awareness of such, does not contain the past. Additionally, Marsh continues, the trace itself—the footprint—has nothing of the original's content, while our long-term memories quite clearly do.

The trace-theory of memory, that an event is preserved neurally as a trace, also fails, Marsh argues, in accounting for the difference in feeling that a long-term memory may have from the original event. If memory were a trace phenomenon, a neural trace reactivation, my recollection of past suffering would have necessarily a feeling of that suffering. Deactivating the trace, then, would be deactivating the memory. However, I can have the memory of an injury without a semblance of injury to myself. The suffering component has been deactivated without extinguishing the memory. This invalidates the trace hypothesis as the neural-memory store, for the semblance of suffering is not retained. If memory cannot be a trace of the original, it cannot be recollected by neural-trace activation.[11]

Removal of brain tissue, whose electro-stimulation elicited reports of long-term memories from the patients involved, does not remove those memories. They remain, but the brain tissue does not. And memory as a neural pathway—whether one call it a groove or a trace—has been shown to explain nothing of memory's existence. Moving to a smaller—or more micro scale, if one wishes—than these larger components of brain matter, advocates of the physical basis of memory's preservation have advanced the suggestion that RNA/DNA events in the cell show this possibility. Memory, that is, has a material substrate.

A. R. Luria, a leading proponent of this view, summarized the hypothesis in The Working Brain[12]

> The quest for a solution to the problem of the material basis of memory took a new turn as a result of the work of Hyden (1960; 1962; 1964) who showed that retention of a trace from previous excitation is associated with a last change in the ribonucleic acid and who found a lasting increase in the RNA/DNA content in nuclei subjected to intensive excitation. In both places RNA/DNA molecules . . . play the decisive role . . . in the retention of traces from previous experience during the life of the individual. At the moment of excitation the RNA level in the neurons rises while that of the surrounding glia falls; whereas in the after-period (evidently connected with trace retention) it falls sharply in the neurons but rises equally sharply and remains high for a long time in the glia. The hypothesis that the glia is concerned in the retention of memory traces is unquestionably one of the most important discoveries in neuro-physiology. . . .

Holger Hyden, working at the University of Goteborg, developed a quite precise microminiaturized method for analyzing the nucleic content of nerve and glial cells. In his experiments Hyden isolated Deiters cells—very large neurons—out of the rat medulla and subjected them to a heavy barrage of nerve impulses. He then compared their RNA content with that of a control group of cells. Subsequently, having shown that this was possible, Hyden presented young rats with the difficulty of walking a thin tightwire to get to their food source. When they had learned how to walk, he compared the RNA content of their Deiters cells with those of control animals which had not learned this tightwire act. The RNA content of the control group was measurably less than the non-control group. Also, the base sequence of the RNA in the control group differed from the non-control group.

Similarly, with planaria (flatworms) the base composition of their cerebral RNA changed upon learning a conditioned response: the quantity of adenine diminished and of guanine increased. Furthermore, the changed RNA was extracted from the conditioned planaria and injected into other flatworms. Their behavior changed as though the conditioned response taught to the first group had been transferred[13]

The change in the molecular structure of neuronal glial cells in the laboratory animals upon their conditioning, or learning, serves for this line of reasoning as evidence of a chemical basis for memory. A change in behavior upon introduction of a stimulus presumably involves a macrochemically- made recall capacity in the organism in that, once the behavior is acquired it need not be relearned. It is now part of the organism's chemistry, its neural composition.

Problematic with this line of reasoning is that it seeks to extrapolate from the activity of behavior modification a thesis that it could then equally apply to an entirely different phenomenon, long-term memory. While behavior modification is a change in behavior due to a certain stimulus, long-term memory involves no behavior modification. But it was behavior modification that the chemical changes in neuronal cells was supposed to explain. If long-term memory is not a behavior modification, the chemical changes involved to explain behavior modification have nothing to do with long-term memory. Citing those changes, accordingly, in the case of long-term memory does nothing to advance our understanding of how long-term memory might be formed. The changes are irrelevant to an inquiry into how long-term memory comes about.

Even if we grant that behavioral modification has a chemical basis, that has not been made evident by those advancing it. If impartial reasoning is how truth is reached, and impartial reasoning means the avoidance of assumptions in favor of letting the data speak for themselves, it is clear that the chemical hypothesis of learned behavior has not proceeded this way.

For example, two changes occurring together, as in the case of neuronal RNA and behavior, do not necessitate that one is the cause of the other. That one is however, must be assumed if the chemical hypothesis is to have any force. At best, only a correlation between the two can be established. A change in neuronal RNA, as ill the case of the rats after walking a tightwire is not evidence that it was the process of learning the tightwire that caused the change. One can equally ask how did the rat first cross the tightwire prior to the RNA change? If the RNA change explains how it learned the tightwire crossing, what explains how it first crossed it? For learn means to come to know how.

To assert that RNA change explains the subsequent and evident facility with which the rat crosses the tightwire after first doing it—or after a number of times—requires that the RNA change be viewed as a cause for quickly, adroitly, crossing the tightwire. A modification in behavior is linked to a chemical change; once the change occurs, the modification follows. This position, however, has difficulties.

If a cause is responsible for the sameness of result each time it is operant, exceptions to that result have to be explained. One would expect that the rat's behavior each time in crossing the tightwire should be the same if it is chemically induced. That, unimpeded, for example, it should take the same number of steps, effect the same bodily movements, cross at the same speed. It does not, though, which leaves one uncertain as to what kind of causality the RNA change is supposed to effect. How does neuronal RNA explain behavior when the behavior in question frequently differs? When is the behavior sufficiently different, or the same, so that one can distinguish between pre- and post-neuronal RNA change, or assert that it is post-neuronal RNA that explains the behavior? Requests for such delineation have not been readily answered by defenders of the chemical hypothesis of behavior.

Applying these canons of evidence to the instance of tissue transplantation and planaria behavior involves similar difficulties. To posit that the RNA tissue transplant from a planarian with behavior X is responsible, after transplantation, for a second planarian's new behavioral trait, is it not necessary to show that the second planarian could behave in no way other than which the RNA change is held to cause? In cases of causality we know that certain effects are not possible from a cause, that instead only one effect is possible. In the case of the planaria we do not know what effects are involved because we have no way of knowing if another behavior, other than the one observed, is possible. And we do not know this because we do not know whether it is the tissue transplant that accounts for the behavior. In this case we would have to prove that no other behavior, other than the one associated with the RNA tissue transplant, was possible. That would satisfy a claim of causality in this case. No such proof is possible, though, while it is proof that is required if one is to be convinced that changes in behavior are RNA-explained. At most, one can only suggest from the evidence that RNA neuronal change might be instrumental to the change in behavior, not causative of it. Some causality is required in a learning change. That is admitted. And that causality could be material. Since a learning change has no connection with long-term memory, that materiality would have no impact, however, on the argument for long-term memory's non-materiality. That notwithstanding, it has not been proven that the material agency causing learning changes is RNA.[14]

Difficulties similar to those besetting the materialist reasoning process that drew conclusions from experiments without data for such conclusions appear in a suggestion from the same quarter: Neuronal synaptic changes may be causative of behavioral changes and memory preservation. It is known in neuroscience that the neuronal cell synthesizes those substances that travel down the axon to the nerve synapse. So in Hyden's findings, and others', e.g., Edward Glassman's, since neuronal RNA changes in the presence of a new behavior it follows that a change in the synaptic conjunction among neuronal cells occurred. In fact this was shown to be the case in electron micrograph studies carried out by Brian Cragg in London.[15] The anatomical change in the synapse is evidence of a material substrate accounting for memory functioning since, the materialist hypothesis maintains, upon acquiring new behavior the synaptic structure changes one way and no further.

The difficulty with this hypothesis is two-fold. (1) In Cragg's work rats were reared in the dark for the first two weeks of their lives and then exposed to laboratory light for three hours before they were killed. Cragg found that changes occurred in both the size and number of synapses in the visual cortex, lateral geniculate, and retinae of these animals. These synaptic changes, however, do not show that learning involves them. They are, in fact, changes one would expect in the presence of new stimuli, given the obvious neurochemical changes that occur in sensation. No connection with learning can be made here unless (2) it is assumed that the synaptic change in neuronal cells that occurs in behavior modification is the basis of an organism's new behavior.

It is the assumption that must be watched. Too much is assumed, too much is not proven, in the conclusion that follows from it. As we saw before, if neuronal cell changes account for a new behavior, how are we to explain the behavior of the rat in first crossing the tightwire? How did it learn this feat initially? The neuronal change affecting learning, behavior, had not yet occurred. If it is because the rat crossed the tightwire more easily after the neuronal RNA change that the RNA change is deemed causal, it is being assumed that without the RNA change the new-found agility would not have arisen. And that has to be proven. It is just as plausible that the RNA recomposition was caused by the rat's learning to cross the tightwire. That position becomes objectionable only on the assumption that learning and behavioral change are chemically caused. And that is the point—that they are chemically caused has to be proven, not assumed.

The point in this review of the scientific claim of a material basis for memory is that this claim has not been demonstrated. An unproved assumption underlies the claim, which we have seen to be the case in other claims advancing a materialist explanation for living existence.

The issue here can be further focused. Learned habits—which is the example used by scientists advancing a material nature for memory—are not, as we already commented, in any manner like the long-term memories whose material basis they sought to establish in their experiments on behavior modification in animals. Acquired habits can be lost through lack of reinforcement. Long-term memories need no reinforcement for their retention. Skill at a certain task, in a certain habit, can be improved. A long-term memory cannot. The basis required for comparison, viz., similarity, between short-tern, memory (habit, behavior modification) and long-term is clearly not present. Their difference is one of essence.

Even dismissing these problems with the scientific claims of a chemical structure to memory, there are improbabilities in their own thesis. If we assume that memories are molecular phenomena, what kind of brain molecules could serve as their basis? They would have to be complex, and thus large enough, to accommodate the high complexity of differences contained in the wide variety of memories we have. The macromolecules within the nerve cell which we could select for this memory role are limited. They would have to be, on the materialist's own grounds, either proteins or the nucleic acids themselves—DNA or RNA, the ribonucleic acid that bears the gene's DNA message and builds the protein molecules. It is these that are the constituents of the nerve cells, what physically comprise them.

Here again the molecular thesis runs into difficulty. All three candidates for memory production use logically equivalent codes. The amino acids' series in a protein possesses information exactly parallel to, indeed identical with, the sequence of bases in RNA on which it grew. And that sequence is simply a translation of the base sequence in the DNA gene. It is much like stating the same sequence in braille, Fortran, and script.

If memory is molecular, each new memory would need a wholly unique protein or RNA molecule to be made so that it could be stored. That, however, would require synthesis of a totally new DNA sequence in the neuronal gene. Since memories are continuously being formed, the change in the DNA sequence would have, concomitantly, to be continuous. There is no evidence, though, that the DNA of nerve cells is constantly changing. Quite the contrary; it is scientific fact that DNA is not continuously being replaced. Just the opposite; it manifests extraordinary persistence and imperviousness to change.[16]

The molecular-basis theory of memory falls, then, on its own requirements. The component cited for memory formation, that is, the molecule—the basic structure of all cellularity—is empirically known to be inadmissible. Neuronal gene DNA, which would have to be the neurological agent in a molecular theory of memory, functions exactly opposite to what the theory requires. As the core agency of all neuronal molecularity, production of memory tissue would require that its own sequence of nucleic acids alter for each new memory-specific molecule. To account for the differences each human memory contains, no memory molecule could be the same as another. Otherwise the memories would be the same. The differences among our memories, their variation in complexity, imagery, information, and structure, would require each a molecule precisely fitted for those differences, as well as the necessary permutations in the sequence of DNA arrangement productive of that molecular fitting. It is those permutations, however, which do not occur, and is known scientifically not to. Thus it is rational, I argue, to conclude that memory cannot be molecular. For the conditions necessary to that molecularity are scientifically known not to exist.

A brain-tissue basis of memory, then, is not supportable on the evidence. From the levels of gross-tissue excision to the molecular the materialist case has not been demonstrated. This means that tissue such as the aforementioned hippocampus or media) thalmus known to be necessary to the formation of memory could not be productive of it. The fact that such tissue is DNA-based shows this. The past cannot be stored as a molecule; we just saw that. To produce memory is to store the past such that it can be recalled to awareness: the action of DNA—its constancy of sequence—makes clear that brain tissue cannot contain it. Each new memory requires a different RNA so that it can be molecularly contained. the permanence of DNA's sequence means that the RNA required to fulfill this task is not being produced. And thus the brain molecule is not.

That DNA does not change or, to say it otherwise, that neuronal cells remain undifferentiated one from another, puts to serious test theories postulating that memory exists in bits stored over various brain sites and assembled for our recall in or by the hippocampus when we wish to remember. Each cell or neuronal cluster would have to change with each bit of memory that it was supposed to encode or encapsulate since each memory-bit itself would be different for different memories. DNA's sameness of neuronal cell production, however, makes that thesis untenable. All memories would have to be the same. Further, assemblage of memory bits assumes prehension of the whole that the parts to be assembled are to comprise. That which is to be remembered is already present to mind, thus eliminating the need for assembly of its constituents. Memory, then, is not preserved in this disaggregated condition among neural clusters. Neurological sites may be physically active in the activity of memory, but clearly they are not its constituents.

Memory, then, is not reducible to a brain molecule. Memory is the storage of the past, a storage, though, that cannot be neurocellular. No brain tissue can produce it, therefore, since to store the past is to produce memory. This means that the necessity of the hippocampus or mesial thalmus to memory's emergence cannot be causative. This holds for any brain tissue whose absence would prevent the formation of memories. If their absence prevents the formation of new memories, it does not follow that those tissues form new memories. Absence of a part followed by absence of an event does not mean that the part is causal to, or suffices for the occurrence of the event. As necessary to storage of the past they must be instrumental in memory's formation, not causative of it. The causality is ruled out because they are governed by DNA.

Brain tissue's instrumentality may be conceived of as that by which the individual missing such tissue could not form any memory as his, and thus not form any memory, because memory always belongs to someone. That by which he would form a memory as his would be missing and thus he would be unable to form a new memory. It is in this that brain tissue's instrumentality to memory's formation can be suggested. It is the instrument for the memory's being mine (because, for example, the mesial thalmus is mine), and therefore for the memory occurring. Parts such as the hippocampus and mesial thalmus are instruments by which an event is prepared for storage such that what is stored uniquely and individually for each person could not be so without these brain parts. The actual storage—what causes the event to be preserved, what preserves it—is beyond their instrumentality. The evidence is that it is not a material process.

This leaves one remaining hypothesis to consider. It is the hologram theory of brain. Can the hologram theory find a place for memory in the brain tissue?

The hologram model of brain received its impetus in neuroscience from Karl Pribam, experimental psychologist at Stanford University, and Christopher Longuet-Higgins of the University of Edinburgh.[17] Essentially, a hologram is a photographic plate whose image data can be resurrected and reconstructed three dimensionally by laser light at any point on that plate. The image-forming property is dispersed throughout the plate, such that the image can be reconstructed more or less from any part broken off the plate.

Such a construct, Pribam suggested, might explain the fact that memories are not extinguished despite the destruction of brain areas whose electrode stimulation evoked them. Memory, the hologram argument runs, is distributed over the brain as a whole in much the way the image of the hologram is enfolded in all of its parts.

The suggestion has drawbacks. It requires that the brain tissue be shown to have those physical properties which make it holographic in the way the photographic plate is when struck by laser light. Is it only a laser light that can generate such a property? If so, what is the analogue for that light in the brain? More directly, how do we show that the analogue can accomplish that for which it is the analogue?

The hologram thesis requires the use of analogical conception to have explanatory power given the differences between the media, namely, the photographic plate and brain tissue involved in the thesis. Between the two there must be some analogue by which those differences are overcome so that there be a similarity remaining that makes intelligible or workable the thesis as it applies to brain tissue.

Beyond that, the analogue, to have serviceability, must be shown to operate similarly in the case of both media. The analogue would have to be "the power of enfoldment" or its equivalent. That precise power in the brain, equivalent to the action of laser on plate, would require that the tissue it act on respond in a fashion similar to that of the photographic plate to laser. The tissue must have similarity enough to the plate's constituency, for this is what analogy requires, to respond holographically. For this requirement we have the physical datum by which to judge the analogy's usefulness. It is the brain tissue itself. Composed ultimately of DNA, RNA, and proteins, it is difficult to fathom how they would exercise properties similar to a photographic plate's components when the photographic plate contains none of the brain's cellular make-up. If the properties of the photographic plate are required in the neuron so that it react holographically, the neuron would have to be so composed that it could exhibit those properties. Empirically, however, we know those properties to occur only through photographic plate constituency. If there is an agency in the brain by which in connection, in interaction, with the neuron it could act as a power of enfoldment, and thus the neuron exhibit the properties of the photographic plate, we have no evidence for it. And a power working on tissue whose molecules cannot contain memories (unlike the photographic plate which in its parts has at least bits of the whole), and yet still is supposed to be able to produce memories in the way of holographic reproduction—appears to be a totally unworkable hypothesis.

We are led back, then, to the original position of this chapter. There is no evidence that long-term memory is a physical result. No scientific experimentation shows it to be equitable with a neurochemical, a biological, component. Long-term memory is not reducible to brain tissue or brain space.

The evidence that memories are retained alter brain tissue, whose electrode stimulation evoked those memories, is removed impairs the brain-storage explanation of memory. The evidence that a more substantial removal leaves memories intact further reduces its plausibility. Clinical removal of suitably complex tissue with memory unaffected argues that memory has no place, no location, in the human brain. Removal of the hippocampal region, as we noted, prevents further memories from being formed. That, though, would simply show that brain region to be instrumental in memory formation. And this no one questions. The memories the person already has, however, the evidence suggests, reside someway other than in the brain tissue. The brain, from what can be empirically shown, is not causal to the memories formed. The notion that the whole is somehow present in the part, and thus memory preservation may be possible that way, requires that the memory be contained in the brain in the first place. Neuromolecularity, however, makes plain that memory cannot be molecular. Regions of the brain possibly not explored in clinical treatment will be shown not to contain memory, for their molecularity requires neuronal DNA, in which regions it plays the same role as in the remaining brain. Examination of the information provided by neuroscience, therefore, as well as its assumptions, rules out memory being in any part of the brain. It exists without place.

This preservation of one's past in one's cognitive apparatus appears to have no plausibility as a material process. Its preservation, rather, emerges as immaterial.

It is worth restating how this assertion comes about. To preserve this past from one's life requires an activity for the one remembering that is not constricted to place. Bodily make-up—histological structure and content—is not whence the represented past is drawn. The past does not stay in the body, does not persist in a material state and then, upon the individual's election, enter awareness.

The responsibility for bodily function is cellular: bodily life is cellularly controlled and based. The past recollected is not cellular. Neuronal DNA's biochemical identity—its sameness of chemical coding and thus cellular production—over the life of the brain eliminates a cellular/molecular role in memory. That precludes retention of the past as a material process at the most constitutive level of the brain, the level of DNA. The most constitutive level of an organism is responsible for what results in or from the organism at any other level when no other factor intervenes. Science has found no other factor of such importance in the cell's constitution for its growth than DNA. Since DNA cannot account for memory, that would rule out a cellular (material) explanation or basis for it. Neuro-electric activity as a possible factor in memory would have somehow to alter the composition of the molecule if the molecule is to be a store for memory. Since the molecular composition of the neuron does not so alter (neuronal DNA being established as the sole agent of neuronal composition), a neuro-electric role in memory appears excluded. Neuro-electric activity would have to be able to alter a (macro) molecule, exercise the same causality DNA can. It is known, however, not to (that is, it provides no cellular code). The known spontaneity and randomness of such charges would equally eliminate them from a role in memory. Memory does not happen sporadically, suddenly; thus it could not be a neuro-electric circumstance.

Memory's retention could appear, therefore, to be immaterially derived. The preservation of the past points to an in-material function in man. In his memories man can suggest a reason to call himself indestructible. Brain death is not demonstrated to be the end of personal existence.

If memory has no place, then it is not necessary for what exists to have place. To think it must is gratuitous, to assume what cannot be proven. Our entire world of material being exists in place; and much, if not all, of what we remember is of that world. It is not extraordinary, then, that we come to think of all existence as placed, and only as such. Nor, given man's proclivity to habit—of thought as well as of action—that he would find dubious the notion of existence without place. In most thought processes a sense-image is the most serviceable vehicle, and that image generally carries with it the representation, content, of place.

If place is a boundary around that which is in it,[18] to think of memory as not in place is to think of it as having no boundary, of not being contained. To so think it is not to conceive it as infinite. Absence of physical boundaries simply means the content of an existent, or the existent itself, does not require place. An infinite existent would require a content that is infinite, as well as absence of physical constraints. Memory does not exist in that way; its content is always finite but, we are saying, not in place.

Though we do not in our everyday thinking picture to ourselves such existence, it is not for that reason unintelligible to us. The absence of sense-imagery in thought processes, e.g., has not been all impediment to convergence theory in mathematics,[19] or the mathematics of Lobaschevskian geometry within a Euclidean framework.[20] In the latter, especially, a mental representation of the unbounded appears as a conceptual apparatus.

Thought in the absence of sense-imagery conveying physical containment is, of course, not a commonplace but is operant when thought penetrates to formalization, as in mathematics. Conceptualizing memory in a non-bounded way reaches a similar level of abstraction. If that level be serviceable in mathematics, ruling it out in how we think about memory appears unwarranted. Thinking of memory in non-bounded terms, therefore, is not an exception that stands out alone in human thought processes. The thesis that long-term memory is an existence not susceptible to material containment, physical boundary, does not lead to an inconceptualizability. Memory can be so conceived. The thesis does not conflict with other thought processes, and has a cognate in areas of mathematics.

That thesis, so formulated, means that human existence appears to possess a capacity not limited to this world of space-time; not everything human has the constraints of materiality. One objection to immortality stemmed from the requirement that survival of death be existence as we know it in this space-time. If existence after death, so the objection went, is not life as we know it while living, post-mortem existence must be rejected.

From all the research, though, memory does not appear emplaced. The objection that post-mortem existence has no validity because it must, like life, be spatio-temporal, assumes something for which it does not have evidence, to wit: that human capacity in this life is only spatio-temporal. The argument from memory should make clear that it need not be. By eliminating the materialist candidates for its explanation at every cellular level of brain tissue, the case for memory's immateriality takes on serious considerability.

It would be a demonstration of that immateriality were the method of excluding possibilities demonstrative in force. In the case of concept formation the principle of excluded middle[21] allowed us to demonstrate the concept's immateriality because the alternative to its materiality was not a variety of other possibilities, but only one, that is, immateriality. In the instance of memory, materialists can suggest some terra incognita that the method of exclusion has not considered. While our procedure of examining all levels of neuronal cellularity has excluded those levels as possible stores for memory, it can be argued that it is not inconceivable that some as yet undiscovered neuronal material or structure may surface to account for the place of long-term memory in the human brain. To that extent the immateriality of memory is not established. Its likelihood, though, has been established if no cellular agent exists overriding and replacing DNA's role in the neuronal gene. DNA in such a circumstance would relinquish its role as the basis of cellularity. To the extent that that is unlikely, the immortalist can argue that memory's immateriality is not.

NOTES

1. Wilder Penfield, *The Mystery of the Mind*, (Princeton, NJ: Princeton University Press, 1975), p. 21.

2. *Ibid.*, pp. 21–22.

3. *Ibid.*, pp. 24–27.

4. Wilder Penfield and Phanor Perot, "The Brain's Record of Auditory and Visual experience: A Final Summary and Discussion" in *Brain*, vol. 86, pt. 4, December, 1963.

5. Duplication of it elsewhere in another temporal lobe site seems unlikely. What would prevent a duplicate recall if it were thus duplicated? And why stop at a duplicate site? What theoretical difference is there between a duplicate or quintlicate (five locations) site of a memory in the brain tissue?

6. See nn. 1 and 4, above.

7. Sir John Eccles, ed., *Brain and Conscious Experience* (New York: Springer Verlag, 1966).

8. Jacques Barbizet, *Human Memory and Its Pathology*, trans. by D. Jardine (San Francisco: W. H. Freeman, 1970).

9. Michael Marsh, *A Matter of Personal Survival: Life After Death* (Wheaton, IL: Quest, 1985), pp. 39–40.

10. *Ibid.*, pp. 43–44.

11. *Ibid.*, pp. 48–53.

12. A. R. Luria, *The Working Brain: An Introduction to Neuropsychology*, trans. by Basil Haigh (New York: Basic Books, 1973), pp. 281–82.

13. C. U. M. Smith, *The Brain: Towards an Understanding* (New York: Putnam, 1970), pp. 321–22.

14. In lower primates (as in macaque monkeys) bilateral removal of the hippocampus and amygdala has prevented remembering events that occurred immediately prior (as briefly as two minutes) to their removal. Their neuronal circuitry to the basal forebrain and its acetylcholine fiber network tot he cortex has prompted the hypothesis that acetylcholine, along with other neurotrans-

mitters, may cause cellular changes in the brain's synapses that harden sensory impressions formed and/or mediated in the brain's neural network into physical deposits called memories. (See Tim Appenzeller and Mortimer Mishkin, "The Anatomy of Memory," Scientific American, [separate monograph], 1987).

We have already seen the difficulty with this trace or groove theory of memory, while it is not clear whether a failure of recognition of an object after an amygdalectomy might not show simply that and not that an object cannot be remembered. Failure to recognize and failure to remember are not the same. Granting, as the neurological data in this case seem to indicate, that this failure to recognize is a failure of memory, that does not show that memory is physically stored. An electric switch, which mediates electric current, does not contain the music its mediation powers. The information for the song, in fact, is on a tape or disc, neither of which is part of the electric switch. The amygdaloid may function in the same way as the switch: remove it and you remove the memory in the same way that, in removing the electric switch you remove the sound of music.

15. See Steven Rose, *The Conscious Brain* (New York: Alfred Knopf, 1973), pp. 197–98.

16. Colin Blakemore, *Mechanics of the Mind* (Cambridge: Cambridge University Press, 1977), pp. 110–11.

17. Steven Rose, *The Conscious Brain*, op. cit., p. 203. See also Michael Talbot, *Beyond the Quantum* (New York: Bantam, 1986), pp. 51–52.

18. See Aristotle, *Physics*, 212a 20.

19. I am thinking of the work of Father Bolzano, Paradoxes of the Infinite, trans. by D. A. Steele, (London: Routledge and Kegan Paul, 1950) and that of Augustin-Louis Launchy.

20. Poincaré, as explained by Carl R. Boyer (*A History of Mathematics*, Princeton, NJ: Princeton University Press, 1985, p. 653), effected a mathematical composition wherein inhabitants of a certain universe would prehend their universe as infinite. Such a universe with these inhabitants is thinkable to us (for no inherent contradiction is entailed), even if not "picturable."

Whether or not such a universe actually exists, i.e., bespeaks an actual infinity, is a metaphysical question. In n. 7 of ch. I I have argued against an actually existing infinite space, and would against Poincaré. My point here is simply that mathematics has not found the notion of unboundedness an inherent constraint to its abstraction. Potential unboundedness, where one is not speaking of an infinity existing altogether, but as that which is always free of any boundaries one chooses, would serve just as well in the Poincaré citation, a citation chosen only to indicate that the notion of existing without boundaries or containment is not exclusive to the profile of memory here being developed.

21. That something either is or is not; alternatively, either is "x" or is not "x."

IV
The Argument from Consciousness

It is no longer fashionable to doubt the existence of a self, an identity of being through one's life amid the changes that pass in that life as rapidly as they arise. "Self" means that there is a permanence about each individual person that is not bodily. There is, according to the notion, an invariant origin of activities intrinsic to the one who undertakes them which gives one a continuity throughout the vicissitudes of life. This invariance remains through every change it accompanies.

A perduring unitive principle of all the individual's operations is what the term "self" means. It is the core constituent of one's uniqueness, the originating ground of individuality functioning through every experience. The self is the beginning of all one's personhood in its incommunicability and inalienability. It is that inimitable presence concurrent with and expressed through each moment of personal existence.

It was the empiricists who challenged the reality of selfhood. Its existence could not be demonstrated, they noted. No premises bring about a proof for it. If the existence of something requires it be demonstrable thus, the existence of the self would have to be denied. It is patently gratuitous, to answer this, to equate assurance of existence with its demonstrability.

Since, further, they held the self could not be an object of sensation, we could not be certain of its existence. The argument questioning the existence of the self assumes that only sense-objects qualify as conduits of knowledge. Only what has sense features, is an object of the sense-faculties, can be considered factual in origin. Any notion, however arrived, that was not traceable to a sense-object was not one that had a verifiable basis. It was without "evidence." Since the self has no sense-features, empiricism concluded, nothing in our conception of it bore the mark of knowledge.[1]

Empiricism's central tenet is that we must be skeptical about any claim not confirmable through the five senses. And as with many claims we have encountered in this book, empiricism's claim that only sense-objects provide knowledge of things is not provable. That all human knowledge of objects is or must be sense-restricted is certainly not a proposition that sense-objects tell us. Nor is there anything about the terms in the empiricist's proposition that establishes the necessity of such relationship: there is nothing about the term "knowledge" that says were it not identical to sensation a contradiction would ensue, i.e., that it would be contradictory if a mental event indicating the possession of truth occurred in the absence of some sense-datum to correspond to that event. This necessity in the relationship of terms or ideas was the only other certainty allowed by the empiricists. Terms were necessarily related to one another if denying a relationship between them resulted in a contradiction. No such necessity appears, here, though, between the terms knowledge and sensation. Nor is it obvious, immediately undeniable, that the empiricist identification of knowledge with sensation is true; or that certainty of mind reached in grasping a necessity of relation among terms is necessarily equivalent to have reached the truth.

Nor can the empiricist, as a defense, ask for a counter-example that would invalidate his proposition that only sense-objects qualify as objects of knowledge. For on his own conditions there is no way to assure the validity of counter-example argumentation. Sense-data do not furnish us with the notion of counterfactual validity. To follow Hume's instructions,[2] if we examine in every detail the sense-features of any object the idea "counter-example validity" cannot be traced to any one of them, or to the relation of sense-features to one another. For the empiricists to ask for a counter-example is to reject their own thesis that certainty is measured only by an object's status as a sense-datum or a proposition's undeniability. Any proposition violating the principle of non-contradiction was untenable; anyone not was deniable, unless there was sense-data to the contrary. Nothing in the notion "counter-example" can be tested by this criterion of undeniability; nothing in our concept includes it. Nor is there anything about the statement "all ideas must be traceable to sense-objects," sense-features, that would make the statement's denial self-contradictory. And there is nothing about sense-evidence or sense-objects that tells us the proposition is undeniable—or even true.

Nothing in the empiricist argument against the idea of self prevents us from asserting the reality of selfhood, then. That it was taken seriously says more about those that so took it than it does about the argument itself.

In positing the existence of the self it is important to distinguish bodily continuity from that continuity of being known by the term "self." In death the body corrupts, so that if we can distinguish selfhood from body bodily dissolution will not necessitate that of selfhood.

The notion of self entails that of perdurance; in our current state that means sameness over a time, a lifespan, that it is to an identical agent to which different events at different times are related. One objection to this notion is that the evidence for this continuity is only the body. This is what constitutes the continuity over time that others refer to as selfhood. Personal continuity, identity, is nothing more than bodily.

The body cannot be the source of the notion of self, of "I," however. Were it, to identify an experience as belonging to me, being mine, would require the body be the criterion for so judging. To use your body as the criterion presumably would require an awareness of your body. But on what grounds could you cite your body as yours since that by which you would do it, sc., your body, you have no grounds in this case for determining is yours? You cannot use the body as the criterion, for it is precisely that whose experience is in question. The point is plain: the body cannot be the basis for the notion of "I," "mine," of "self."

It is perhaps memory that gives rise to our conception of self, that perduring spring of individual agency and personhood. To perceive at time "B" that an event at time "A" in the past happened to you requires that in some way you be identical in both, that that to whom "A" and "B" happened be identical. Otherwise the individual to whom "A" happened could not, contrary to what our experience is, be that individual at "B." If you are not the same in both instances, you could not say that the individual at time "B" was the individual to whom "A" occurred.

We do, though, have awareness of a personal past, an awareness that is immediate, without need of proof, that "A" and

"B" are linked for a consciousness. Through this awareness I perceive that something about me endures, that I have a continuity transcending the separate experiences of life. Through memory I come to the realization of an identity to my existence through every experience. Memory is direct prehension of the past, not a reasoning process by which something is proved as past. Through memory I come to grasp that something about me in life is never different. There is a sameness about me, to which it points, permeating all the differences through which I have existed.

In this realization it is not that I deliberately pause and reason that since memory points to a perdurance about me over time I therefore enjoy selfhood. It is when thinkers have to defend the notion of 'self' that a reasoning process along these lines is used. Our awareness about it seems to be almost a direct one, i.e., an unreflective realization.

If it is memory that indicates selfhood, gives rise to the notion, to undermine that notion's validity requires challenging the veracity of memory. This is not feasible, though, since any challenge to memory requires memory's veracity. Even pointing to memory's fallibility requires a veracity about memory. This would appear to make the grounds for the assertion of selfhood reasonable.

This intangible sameness of agency, then, is that to which we give the term 'self'. More than a verbal convenience, more than a mere grammatical structure, more than an empty receptacle; it is what makes everything I do "mine," and what differentiates me from every other person in his role as agent. It is how I exist in the world: I would not be who I am unless it were as this self.

The self appears in the world as both subject and object. We have argued already for its non-bodily reality by excluding bodily continuity from the meaning of 'self'. As an object, my selfhood is never known directly by others. Nor is their's an object of direct acquaintance for me. Awareness of other selves is through a process of inference and analogy. I as a self act in a certain way; others similarly act. To do so they must possess a causal agency, a power of activity, equivalent to mine. But my causal agency is one of selfhood. To those about whom I can make this judgment I attribute the character of selfhood. The admitted inability to possess that certitude about such judgments where denying that other individuals are selves would not be contradictory should not be as troublesome as it is to thinkers who need that kind of certitude. Eminent reasonableness about some conclusions must often suffice for intelligent discourse. If a situation does not admit of the kind such as some want for our conclusion about other selves in the world, it might just be inappropriate to ask for that kind of certitude. Not every truth is demonstrable; nor is every correct judgment the result of inferential reasoning. The incredulity expressed at the possibility that fellow acquaintances might not possess the character of selfhood is a tacit recognition of this.

As a self I exist also as a subject—a consciousness to which events happen and which has through that consciousness experiential contact with the world. That contact is constituted irreducibly by an otherness from that of which I, as subject, am conscious. That point is very important, for from it arises further underpinning for the assertion of man's immaterial status.

My consciousness can never be an object for others. It is a unique perception of the world in which no other consciousness may participate. It has no sense-qualities, is without dimension, and has no location. Where, e.g., in the brain is consciousness of table? And how big is it? How is it, further, that the consciousness of table does not possess the resistance table has when I move against it? Do the brain cells take on this resistance quality? Quite unambiguously they do not, which raises the question how the perception of resistance arises if the perception has no similarity to the nature of brain tissue (which is soft) where the sensation of resistance, hardness, is supposed to be registered. Granting that neurochemical processes and changes correlate with conscious states, how can they be the cause of states that they are totally unlike, from which they are in every respect different? Neurochemical processes, e.g., do not become hard, table-like, in consciousness of the table. Might it be that as the notes of a musical score correspond to, but do not cause, beautiful sounds, the electrochemical events of the brain may correspond to, but do not cause, changes in awareness, perception?

It is a common materialist tenet that electro-chemical events do cause awareness, indeed, that they wholly explain it. Or that they are the conscious experience itself. The tenet has recently been reiterated in Paul Churchland's *Matter and Consciousness*.[3] Each percept (conscious event) is a neural occurrence, or neurally caused. Neural reverberations in the brain set in process by external stimuli constitute human perception. To explain the sense-perception's occurrence in consciousness, neural activity of the brain—its electro-circuitry and topography—as occasioned by the stimulus (the "external" object in the world) is wholly sufficient. In fine, sensation is a material event because the neural activity of the brain is. This would follow from the overall materialist view that consciousness is the activity of suitably organized matter.

To respond, one might consider possibilities or alternatives that result from the thesis that consciousness is reducible to neural activity, the brain's electro-chemical operations. They would divide into the view that the percept is either a material replication, likeness, of external stimuli, or is not a replication at all. Instead, the percept is either the neuro-electric event, or a *product* of it. In considering the different shades of these alternatives the reduction of consciousness to neural activity, which is to say electrical or chemical brain processes, will be shown to be incompatible with consciousness as it actually occurs.

Accordingly, if the percept is the neural event, i.e., if it is material, can it be so as a material reproduction of the original as, e.g., in the manner of the mirror or photographic plate? The electrical firings of the brain upon stimulus are known to be sporadic and unpredictable, thus eliminating them as neural reproductions of the original. Certainly no percept presents itself as such a cacophony. Neurochemical processes appear likewise to be ruled out, for the bonding of chemical compounds bears no resemblance to our percepts. The replication hypothesis as a material facsimile of the original appears to have no basis.

On the other hand, if saying the neural event is the percept means that the percept is a product of the neuro-electrical disturbances in the brain, the hypothesis would be claiming that the neuro-electrical charges interact with one another and by that interaction the percept arises. Different stimuli send different impulses, different data. And the interaction of these disunified impulses from the different stimuli produce the percept. The impulses from the stimuli for height individually interact with those from width and breadth, color, texture, and so on; and the interaction from these impulses together blend and bind precisely for the percept to resemble the object.

Take in this case just the train of impulses from height. Together these impulses through their interaction of electro-charges and field generate the percept of height. That would be a materialist way of arguing that our percepts must originate from the brain's neuroelectrical activity.

To consider it, conceptually take one impulse. It would not be in interaction with any other since we are considering only one. It obviously does not effect the percept height. Otherwise, we would have thousands, if not millions, of that percept since the impulses from the object's stimulation are neurophysiologically known to be of countless number.

If one impulse separately does not generate the percept "height," could the interaction of thousands or millions? We can consider this first exclusively in terms of the electrical interaction itself without reference to any other agency. The interaction of these impulses would have to block out the separate impulses of height information so that we did not have thousands of that percept in one conscious event of an object that had height. But it is from these impulses that the interactions that are blocking them come. This is impossible, however; if the impulses are being blocked they could not cause the electrointeraction; but in the hypothesis it is these that are blocking the impulses. The result is that while they are being blocked there is nothing blocking them—which is impossible.

If the percept cannot be the bombarding successive "info-bits," "info-impulses," is there instead therefore through some other means a grouping of these "info-impulses" that is preserved and held stable in a steady state? This would accord with the percept's status as a stable and coherent content. If there is, it could not be the product of neuroelectric charges. They are neither steady nor unchanging.

Graphing of the brain's neuro-electric activity suggests this. In the study of neural activity in cases of learning performance, EEC (electro-encephlograph) activity has been one means of recording neuronal operation. The transmission of impulses from and through neuron clusters in the brain register on the EEC as electrical waves. These waves are the sum of post-synaptic potentials, i.e., the result of stimuli triggering brain neuroreceptors. These receptors react electrochemically to data when sufficiently stimulated, and register on the EEC in Hz frequency. The undulation (technically, desynchronicity) of these waves shows that the source of these neuro-electric charges is not steady. Neuro-electric activity is not recorded as a straight line, but as

choppy, closely placed lines or segments. This points to an inter-
mittent buildup of synaptic potential and then transmission
release (electrical output) in continual succession. Simply, there
is, as the EEC line undulations show, an inconstancy in neuro-
electrical operations, a transience toward transmissions associated
with the conscious event.

This transience of electrical charge, the suddenness of its
emergence and decline as graphed on the EEC, points to its momentariness in the charge's force. The charge is not a static,
unchanging power lasting in a uniform strength, but a presence
without continuity. While stimuli from the object may be in a continuous wave, and not granulated and discrete particles striking
the sense organ, the synaptic transmission the stimuli cause is not
a steady flow of electrical potential, a continuum or uniformity of
charge. Nerve impulses (neurochemicals converted to such at
each nerve ending release) travel by way of a build-up release conductivity where some data are synaptically inhibited, others not.
Synaptic transmission is a series characterized by the abrupt repetition of electrical rise and fall, of inconstant electrical signals, or
impermanent charges that decline as quickly as they arise. These
features are all expressed by the term 'momentary'.

The percept shows no such rise and fall of force or intensity as
its data are received by the sensory apparatus. Fixed on the object
whose stimuli are even, there is no undulation to the image, or
feature of ebb and flow to the content. The sum of synaptic
potential does not register as sudden transmission-states of informational content, but as a coherence of uninterrupted data
transmission characterized by a smoothness and uniformity of
presence. Neural electrical activity, the operation of momentary
units of force, therefore cannot be the percept's presence in
human sentience. What characterizes it does not characterize
consciousness. What the percept requires, that is, conditions for
continuity, wholeness, uninterruptedness, coherence and
constancy, neural activity cannot supply.[4]

Could the percept's duration derive from a succession of elec-
trocharges in the brain that are somehow made continuous, thus
cancelling their successiveness, their interruptedness? This being
made continuous could not be the work of the brain's electrical
impulses. Since they are discontinuous, i.e., exist only momentar-
ily, they could not effect the continuity that the percept shows
itself to require. Continuity is not momentary; it does not exist in
the moment.

Is some one grouping, instead, selected that excludes the barrage of impulse groupings, in which particular grouping the electrointeraction will constitute the percept? If it is, it cannot be the electrointeraction that emerges in this grouping of impulses which does the selection; for then it would pre-exist itself. And if the percept resembles the original, to select over other groupings one grouping of electro-impulses whose electro-interaction of impulses is to constitute the percept would require awareness of what the original looked like so as to ensure that the right grouping was selected for the percept that results. That awareness, however, would require a prior percept. Electro-interaction could not account for that percept. We have already seen the impossibilities that result when suggesting that the percept in consciousness is the electro-interaction in neural brain tissue, or its product. It must simultaneously both block and receive the data it is blocking; it must be a source of continuity while it itself has no continuity; or it must result from stimuli in which other impulse groupings in the brain's electrical interaction from those stimuli must be excluded by apparently what cannot, as we have said, be electrical. What is not neuro-electrical, however, would go contrary to the materialist identification of consciousness with neural activity, the reverberations of electrical discharges in the brain.

We may consider another example. Take the experience of color. Color is electro-magnetic waves of different length. With chemical changes in the retinal cones caused by these waves reaching the eye, and subsequent neuro-electric activity in the brain's visual cortex via the optic nerve comes the experience of the waves as "color." There are, e.g., nerve fibers that register only the frequency for red. With registration in the visual cortex we have the experience of "red."

If electro-chemical processes produced the percept "red color" they would have to convert the discrete electrical impulses from the wave quanta that have been registered that way because of synaptic conductivity into the uniform percept we have of red. There would have to be an organization of numberlessly successive synaptic inputs, charges, into a coherent, seamless whole. Such organization neuroelectric activity cannot do. Its momentariness and successiveness of occurrence rule it out as the source of continuity and wholeness.

Could continuity in the percept be the work of a hierarchy of neurons? In such a setting this hierarchy would correspond to an electrical grid and, as indicated by the term 'grid', there would be electrocharge build-up. Assuming a hierarchy of neurons, e.g., in the visual cortex (left and right), this movement in electro-charges would represent greater information levels. The continuity in our percept might be traced through this network of build-up. The different levels and types of sensory data and their complexity involve this neuronal hierarchy which, corresponding to different levels of awareness, a neuronal power grid for each sense power (not just sight) can be posited. The neurons may be arranged so that in higher complexity levels of their arrangement they may represent higher capacities for information; and with this level of complexity may be associated a capacity of neural electrical charge build-up. With this hypothesis there is a hierarchical ordering of neurons (in the example "red" the hierarchy being the visual-cortex grid) which, when receiving the lower-level neuronal impulse, becomes with it a higher electrical charge.[5]

Provisions for continuity in our percept are absent in a neural grid, though. In the build-up from lower to higher-level, the prior or lower level no longer exists. When absorbed into a higher neural grid impulse the lower level impulse ceases. It is no longer the level it was. It is subsumed into a higher-level grid charge in virtue of that higher grid's more complex structure (more numerous neuronal arrangements). As the stimulus's electro-charge continues its movement, that higher neural grid impulse ceases to exist at the next level of neuronal complexity that electro-charge engages for the same reason the level prior to it did. This is the route of the stimulus's electrical potential: The build-up of neural electrical charges is a train of impulses which, upon their higher-grid condition, no longer exists continuous with their prior levels—because these levels no longer exist.

They do not because as the electro-charge has coursed upwards its charge at a lower neural grid no longer exists at that level. The lower level has been subsumed into and absorbed to the greater complexity of the neuronal network. That would be the conduct of electrical potentials in a grid format. As such, the lower (or, which is to say the same, prior) level no longer exists for any succeeding (higher) level to be continuous with it. The continuity for the build-up—which is what the percept requires—does not exist then. The mechanism of neuronal charge build-up will not produce the feature that characterizes the percept.

Perhaps there is a sensory threshold that cannot register the successiveness of the stimulus's quanta as they come into contact with the sense organ, and it is this that accounts for our experience of these quanta as a unitary percept. This sensory threshold, it might be suggested, preconditions awareness so that what is perceived has no resemblance to the momentariness of the impulses caused by the object's sense stimuli. That would rule out the need for an organization or synthesis of discontinuous stimuli. If there is such a threshold, it could not be neuro-electric in nature. Such a threshold would require a constancy of force or existence so that certain stimuli (those it blocks out) are not received or registered. Neuro-electric activity, however, is inconstant. It is never permanent.

On the matter of visual perception Sir John Eccles has argued consonantly. Even if we find those "feature recognition" neurons to which each feature in our visual percept is proportioned, how do you get, he asks, the overall composite unity from the discrete data of light, color, depth, form? "The best we can do in neurophysiology is the feature extraction performance observed in neurons of the inferotemporal lobe. . . . Cell after cell can be discovered with selective response at this level of simple geometrical features. This performance is tremendously remote from the vivid picture that is impressed on our retina and which we experience at the end of all this cerebral processing."[6] "We are told that the brain 'sees' lines, angles, edges, and simple geometrical forms . . . . But this statement is misleading. All that is known to happen in the brain is that neurons of the visual cortex are caused to fire trains of impulses in response to some specific visual input. . . . Neurons corresponding to various complications of this specific visual input are identified, but there is no scientific evidence concerning how these feature-detecting neurons can be subjected to the immense synthetic mechanism that leads to a brain process that is 'identical' with the perceived picture."[7]

In the absence of conclusive data, theorists have constructed a model for how to imagine the brain's role in the act of consciousness. The role of the scientist is to offer explanations, and he will do so at times in the absence of evidence. This is not to be faulted so long as it is recognized that the explanation is only hypothesis.

How the theorist will view neurobiological events tends to be determined beforehand by predisposition to explain every event in reductionist or materialist terms. Every event must be materially reducible, for matter explains everything. No experiential state has any other explanation.

Predispositions, however, may get in the way of evidence. In theorizing on the brain's role in awareness it may lead to impossible consequences. In current theory, disaggregated sensory input requires neural synthesis—a material operation—to account for our percepts. If, though, the percept resembles the original, this materialist view fails. Synthesis, by way of which the percept comes to resemble the original, presupposes an awareness of the original prior to synthesis. On the materialist view, however, it is only by the neural synthesis of sensory electro-data that awareness, the percept, occurs. Prior to synthesis a percept is required, but it is only by way of synthesis that a percept comes about. The result is that what is required for consciousness, namely, the synthesis and the percept, never come about. Therefore consciousness cannot. The hypothesis that requires synthesis of sensory electro-inputs to account for consciousness ends up explaining nothing, since consciousness cannot result from those requirements.

This resemblance condition that we have cited means that awareness has a basis outside the perceiving subject, viz., the object its content resembles. The visual percept we have of a tree, for instance, has in it an awareness of a particular spatial pattern that is confirmed by the sense of touch. That is confirmed especially when unintentionally knocking into it. We feel a resistance in such an instance, a being acted against that indicates powerfully the existence of a world outside our consciousness. That resistance confirms what the visual percept conveys when I see the tree as both thick and dense. Experiential grounds asserting resemblance of percept to object appear quite intact then. What is given in the visual percept is confirmed by another sense-faculty. This resemblance of percept to object, however, as we saw above, ruled out the possibility that our percepts result from synthesis of neural data. In the example of the tree, experiential grounds, in which comparison among sensory inputs gives support to the resemblance hypothesis, we are saying, are what rule out the possibility of neural synthesis because of the impossible consequences the condition of resemblance would impose upon neural synthesis.

Absent this condition of the percept's resemblance to the original, i.e., even assuming there is no resemblance to the original, materialism cannot account for consciousness. Its view of the neural events, events that no one denies are associated with consciousness, makes this plain. The materialist view that neuro-electric impulses or their interaction are the equivalent of consciousness is untenable. To account for the unitariness of our percepts, the barrage of electroimpulses in the brain from sensory input have to be explained away. While our percepts are stable and coherently whole, these impulses are chaotic and discontinuous. We saw, however, that they could not be eliminated by the action of neuro-electric impulses, for it is these that have to be eliminated. Nor could the continuity of our perceptual states result from neuro-electric activity, given that activity's momentariness. The material factors, that is, neuro-electric charges, that the materialist cites as explanatory of consciousness cannot explain consciousness. Were those the factors, consciousness could not occur the way it does. As those factors are, they make consciousness impossible. The materialist explanation of consciousness, therefore, would make consciousness impossible.

Again, the impulses from the brain's neural circuitry could not constitute the percept, whether one argues it is the arrangement of such impulses or their system of firings. Such a position is advanced by, among others, Dennet in his *Consciousness Explained.*[8] Electrical impulses, however, are simply flows of electrons and, as such, are always the same in content. No impulse differs from any other in this stream of covalence that makes for electrical charge. Percepts, however, since they are always different, could not be constituted by that which is always the same (that is, they, like the electrical charge, would always have to be the same). A "system" or arrangement of what is always the same has the same difficulty. How determines where one arrangement (percept) ends and another begins if nothing in whatever arrangement you choose can serve to differentiate it from any other arrangement, since what comprises all the arrangements is always identical in each arrangement? These objections suggest the difficulties confronting these who propose computer software as an appropriate model for human consciousness. Clearly the computer can not have percepts. Data is programmed into a computer via chips which, upon electrical power and the appropriate instruction, provide the information desired to whomever is accessing the computer. The computer does not form, does not fashion, the data, however. It is prepackaged for it by way of its software. Human consciousness, arises, though, through percepts fashioned by sensory interaction with the world. We are not born prepackaged with the percepts we will have during life. And we have already seen that electrical impulses cannot be percepts. Outside of its software, however, these are the only informational factors in a computer. The process of exclusion, accordingly, rules out percepts as a computer event.

Further weakening the materialist hypothesis of sense-awareness is the materialist argument from cortical elector-stimulation. Epileptic patients, in the course of neurosurgery, have voluntarily been in a non-invasive and benevolent manner the subject of such cortical stimulation.

Take, for example, electro-stimulation of the cortex with the sense of sound being reported. The materialist cites this as evidence that the sense-event must be material. That assertion requires, however, that one assume that the material impulse— the electrode stimulation—caused the sense-event, i.e., that the electrode stimulation and neuronal structure (its entire histology) potentially contained in its entirety the very result their interaction is said to have caused. Clinically what we observe is an electrode stimulating the cortical area with the patient reporting a sense of sound. To claim from this that the reported sense-event must therefore be material requires one to assume that all interactions must be material. And this is precisely what must be proven for the materialist hypothesis to be true. At the most, in this case all that is known is that the electrode stimulation was the occasion of the percept "sound"— not that it caused the sense-event reported.

Concommitantly, electrode stimulation of neural tissue that impairs awareness does not show that nerve tissue (its composition or interaction with sense data) causes awareness. The most one can argue from this is that such impairment shows neural tissue to be a necessary condition for such an awareness. The point at issue, however, is whether neural tissue is both a sufficient and necessary condition for awareness. Only if it is both can the materialist hypothesis be correct. And we have already argued that the materialist necessity for neural synthesis in the case of each percept renders impossible a causal role to the brain in any percept. And also, beyond that problem of synthesis, that brain activity, since it is electrical, is insufficient for the percept's occurrence.

An ingenious, but upon analysis, flawed argument for the materiality of awareness involves the notion that nerve cells are highly specific. J. Z. Young has suggested that "the discovery of single nerve cells that respond only to a face raises the possibility that neurons may act as code representations of words. This would agree with the way one is apt to lose access to a single word or name—or even a second language ability."[9] In the case of the loss of language ability it is known that sometimes in an individual who is multilingual brain damage is accompanied by the loss of ability in one of the languages the person possessed prior to the brain damage. From that it is argued that neuronal cells specific to that language (its words) were destroyed, causing the subsequent disability. Eliminate neuronal cells specific to Russian, e.g., and the ability at Russian will be lost. Conversely, the implication is that without the neuron the thought or word it "encodes"[10] would be impossible to mention because there was no neuron specific to the thought or word now that the neuron-specific cell was destroyed. The neuron operation becomes the thought. The neuron is a material entity. Therefore, a presentation such as Young's would lead us to conclude, the thought is.

To argue that neurons are stimulus specific is to claim that a neuronal cell—or a minute set of neuronal cells—will respond to only a specific stimulus and no other. Take the case of faces that Young cites.[11] For a neuron or small set of neurons to respond to a face (say face A) would mean they were face-A specific. They would not respond, on this theory, to B, C, D, E, for that would go against the meaning of the term "specific." (In the case of facial recognition, according to proponents of the view, it appears from primate experiments that 19 neurons are involved.) To say that the neuron (or set of 19 of them) was face-A specific is to suggest that Nature beforehand knew what face A would look like and made a set of neurons in the brain—or a neuron itself— stimulus specific to that fact, and placed it in the perceptual apparatus of each and every human. That is a dubious notion. So is the hypothesis derived from it that for each word there exists a word-specific neuron. It is as if Nature knew the Russian language, e.g., and placed in the brain those neurons whose stimulus specificity would account for one's ability in Russian, i.e., for each of its words.

Stimulus-specific neurons are said to "encode" the word which is why, for the materialist, when they have been destroyed knowledge of the language is lost. The encodement, when activated by other neural machinery, is what accounts for language ability. The inference to be drawn from the neural encodement thesis is the materiality of all varieties of percepts, implied by the thesis' suggestion of the possibility of neuron specificity for each cognitive/perceptual datum. Without the neuron-specific brain cell (or cell set) for each experience there would be no experience. Since the neuron-specific brain cell is material in being, experience must therefore be.

While we have presented conceptual difficulties with the neuron specific thesis, the overriding point to be made about it is the distinction of necessary versus sufficient condition. The wheel of a bicycle, for instance, is a necessary condition for the bike's movement. The wheel, however, does not cause the bike to move. Some other agency is required; the wheel is not a sufficient condition for bike travel. In the case of neuronal impairment followed by language failure, a similar reasoning applies.

That is, assume for the sake of argument that the neuron-specific thesis has no conceptual difficulties but instead is correct. One cannot infer from that the reducibility of awareness or language ability to material structures or changes in the brain.

The necessity of living neural tissue to interactive awareness with the world is beyond any dispute; it is well-nigh incontestable. So, however, is the necessity of the wheel to a bike's motion. Is living neural tissue, however, sufficient to that awareness or language ability such that no other factor need be invoked to account for it? This is what the materialist must prove if he is to be convincing in his argument that the absence of language ability after the destruction of brain tissue known to be operant in it means that language ability is totally material in its origin and causality. Noting the absence of language ability after the destruction of brain tissue does not demonstrate the sufficiency of that tissue, however, to language ability. Its sufficiency must be assumed for the inference to follow that therefore language ability is material in its being.

The viscious slip from language ability to its identity with conceptualization, conceptualizability, by Young[12] brings this issue into sharper focus. We have argued in chapter two that certain of our thoughts, concepts, exhibit a feature, namely generality of content, that cannot be materially caused. Language ability as a material occurrence would require that concepts must be material in being if the identity between language and conceptualization is to hold.

Words are not concepts, however. They do, of course, extend our familiarity with concepts we have not ourselves previously formed in that in learning new words we are introduced to the concepts they represent. For letters on a page or a vocal utterance to have meaning for us they must have a content beyond the letters or utterance. They derive their usefulness from the cognitional content they are meant, as media, to convey. Language, then, the written or spoken word, is not identical to conceptualization. I can have a concept without the word (i.e., the written symbol[s] or vocal utterance) because it is the role of the word to point me to the concept it is meant to convey. The content of that concept does not come from the word, but from the item about which it is the concept.

Because we use words as vehicles to convey our thoughts, we are very easily led to identify words with thoughts and knowledge with language. Clearly characteristic of the human species is its thinking by way of the rules of a language. Sentences are the work of those rules. Sentence structure differs in German and English because the languages differ in their rules for that structure. Differences in rules of expression, however, are not differences for the rules of thought content. What governs the content of our thinking and how we think about things are the beings or situations about which we are thinking. How an event is expressed sentencewise—what the grammatical rules for sentence formation are—does not alter how we think about it. It could do so only if the rules for sentence structure were also the rules governing how the event occurred.

Language—the rules and forms of the written or vocal communication of what we are thinking—is not equivalent to human thinking. Differences in language need not be differences in knowledge. The distinction, accordingly, that we made before between the necessary and sufficient conditions of language ability, reappears. If the thought process in this act of conceptualization manifests features that cannot be materially caused, all the more evident is the insufficiency of a thesis that fails to make this distinction between language (its words) and conceptualization; and, as a result, argues that the absence of a language ability after the destruction of brain tissue is ground for identifying the ability to conceptualize as material in its being. Neurons, indeed, could be word-specific. Allow that, as we said before, the difficulties we noted then notwithstanding. Since, however, they are material in being they are not thought-specific. The power of conceptualization is not bound to the existence of neurons. The thought content of our words is not reducible to their role in the brain. They are insufficient in its formation. Thus, while words could indeed be neuronally "encoded," and the destruction of the encoding neurons could be accompanied by the loss of language ability, the loss of those neurons does not necessitate the inability to form thoughts, some of which thoughts in this case have been communicated through the language lost. An inability to form thoughts could be concluded only if there were an identity between thoughts and the words of a language; or, to put it otherwise, only if neuronal encodement were both a necessary and sufficient condition for human thought.

Conceptualization, as a non-material occurrence, makes the encodement thesis doubtful since encodement equates word-specific neurons with thoughts: neurons are thoughts, concepts are brain-cell-set activities. If thoughts were impossible without words (vocal utterances or written symbols), there would be life in Young's suggestion. Words, though, are labels, designations, for our thoughts. They are not the content of them. They are not identical to them. Were vocal utterances or written symbols thoughts, whoever came up with a new utterance or symbol would have come up with a new thought. It is obvious, however, that not every symbol or utterance is a thought. What would indicate a thought function for a symbol or utterance is that symbol or utterance having a referent. That property suffices to establish the distinction we have identified between thoughts and words. You can have a mental prehension of that referent to which the word applies without the word's presence in your mind. Conversely, hearing a vocal utterance or seeing a symbol may convey no thought. That serves to distinguish word from concept or thought, and thus to render at least doubtful J. Z. Young's neuron encodement hypothesis—the equation of word—specific neurons (brain cell sets) with thoughts.

The work of Libet in cutaneous perception further weakens the materialist case for sense awareness. It is reported by Eccles. Simply put, Libet's results show that sensations from stimuli applied simultaneously to body parts responsible for the same sensation (here an electrode to the cortex region associated with hand sensation and another to the hand part associated with that cortex region) were not indicating a disassociation of sensation and physical stimulus. They should both have occurred at the same time if stimulus (neurochemical change) and sensation were identical. That they were not synchronous implies sensation and stimulus (the electrode's application to the cortex, which effects simultaneously a neural change) are not reducible to each other, and therefore that sensation might not be wholly neurophysiological.

> The experiments of Libet on the human brain . . . show that direct stimulation of the some aesthetic cortex results in a conscious experience after a delay as long as 0.5s. for weak stimulation, and similar delay is observed for a sharp, but weak, peripheral skin stimulus . . . although there is this delay in experiencing the peripheral stimulus, it is actually judged to be much earlier, at about the time of cortical arrival of the afferent output. . . . This antedating procedure does not seem to be explicable by any neurophysiological process.[13]

> The cortical activities evoked by some sharp stimulus to the hand in conscious human subjects look as long as half a second to build up to the level for giving consciousness; yet the subject antedated it in his experience to a time which was the time of the arrival of the message from the periphery onto the cerebral cortex, which may be almost half a second earlier. This is an extraordinary happening, and there is no way in which this can be explained by the operation of the neural machinery.[14]

The differences in the timing of the sensation would suggest a severance of neurophysiological change (i.e., the stimulus) from the conscious event (the sensation). The reductionist equation of the two, and thus of consciousness with materiality, is faced in Libet's work with an empirical instance that does not allow for the equation to be drawn. One, because simultaneity is absent, thus disidentifying stimulus with consciousness. And two, because of that absence, the stimulus's causal role would emerge as problematic for the reductionist given the simultaneity that cause and effect require.[15]

Dennet and Churchland[16] for their part have challenged Libet on the length of the antedating time interval (Churchland declaring it, from the work with other participants, to be less). That, however, sidesteps Libet's implication that any lag in reporting invites explanation by means other than material, given the simultaneity of cause and effect. That time interval is the point at issue, while between cause and effect no time can elapse if an effect is coterminus with its cause. Dennet in this regard has suggested that there may be different neuronal "times," say "cortical" versus "limbic" (for the hand), each with its own threshold requirements or "neuronal" adequacies for awareness. Perhaps there are different awareness build-up periods neuronally pre-set that explain the time disparities.

That would argue for identical sensations being generated through different time spans with the same stimulus. That, however, is a case of equal effects issuing from different causes (namely, different time periods), differing factors (those time periods) causing identical results (the sensation of hand tingling). Different causes, however, do not generate identical effects, just as different premises do not yield identical conclusions. That reading of Dennet would put to question his suggestion on limbic versus cortical time. The suggestion does not explain how the sensation is caused in the first place. Libet's findings, surely, however brief the antedating interval appears, remains, then, still an unanswered challenge to reductionism.

Other findings complicate the materialist hypothesis. It is known that some human beings suffering from hydrocephalus— individuals with profoundly diminished brain tissue—have succeeded both academically and socially.[17] In such cases these individuals have a grossly reduced cerebral mantle; ventricle expansion fills 95% of the cranium, which is filled mainly with cerebrospinal fluid. Normal brain tissue associated with sense-input has been compromised in these individuals, forcing doubt about the accuracy of neural mapping. If consciousness is associated with neural reverberations in one brain area, and these reverberations cannot occur with the compromised brain tissue of the hydrocephalic, it is clear that the neural activity in that area, when uncompromised, does not produce consciousness. Nor is it consciousness. For there is normal awareness in these hydrocephalic humans while their brain tissue, whose different areas are supposed to be the sites of consciousness, has been compromised. This, though, violates current neurophysiological doctrine which holds that impaired brain sites should mean impaired intellection and functioning.

Even granting redundancy of brain tissue, where one healthy area of the brain is hypothesized to take up the neural functioning of a damaged area, the problem is not resolved. Left unanswered is the absence of such redundancy in the remaining cases of hydrocephalus. To say in cases where hydrocephalus does not have its devastating effects that redundancy of brain tissue is the reason why it does not, and in cases where it does that there is no redundancy, is not explanatory at all. The redundancy thesis could be useful only if it could account for why redundancy did not occur in those cases in which it did not. The reply cannot be that in those cases something in the brain tissue inhibited redundancy from occurring, since one then has to ask what it is about redundancy that would make it inoperant in those cases. By definition, though, redundancy means that those factors which should make particular brain areas ineffective as the site of consciousness have been overcome. We should not have to ask, then, what it is about brain tissue that would prevent redundancy from occurring, because redundancy is the theory meant to explain why the failure to possess normal consciousness—which the brain-tissue prevention of redundancy would cause—does not occur.

So-called "split-brain" experiments also muddle the materialist hypothesis. Severing the corpus callosum (known as cerebral commisnurotomy) to relieve epileptic distress involves disconnecting neural fibres relating the right and left hemispheres of the brain. In the journal *Neurology* (1977)[18] Donald Wilson and others reported the case of a patient who, upon recovery from this surgery, exhibited two "consciousnesses." The left hemisphere had likes and goals totally different from the right. In sum, the left hemisphere was sufficient for awareness, an awareness coinciding with its goals and views; and the right likewise.

Consciousness in this case seems to need only half a brain such that redundancy of brain tissue is not an operant explanation. No brain areas were removed save possibly remnants of nerve fiber from the severance of the corpus callosum. In this circumstance of bicameral splitting there are two sets of awareness, each with far less brain tissue than was present in the original awareness.

From this clinical case the question arises as to precisely what the quantity of brain tissue must be for consciousness; or if there is any relationship to tissue quantity at all. As the instances of bicameral splitting and hydrocephalus indicate, the relationship between brain tissue and consciousness is much less certain than the materialist doctrine has allowed.

In the case of impaired brain tissue, how is the adjustment made so that consciousness remains unimpeded? Is it by way of some brain mechanism, some neural activity? Is there some neuro-receptor mechanism which is in interaction with all brain areas and through neural electrical messages it receives or fails to receive from different brain areas, brain tissue impairment is detected, with subsequent messages to other brain areas sent to compensate for this impairment? If there were, the difficulty the question of brain tissue quantity presents to the materialist interpretation would lose force. With a neuro-receptor mechanism explaining how brain-tissue impairment is overcome, the materialist interpretation of consciousness could still claim plausibility, whatever the outcome of the question of tissue quantity, since this neuro-receptor mechanism would be material in nature.

It has a difficulty, however, which is a variation of the one we saw in the redundancy thesis. If the ability to overcome brain-tissue impairment is said to be part of the individual's brain composition, to say in the cases that do not overcome this impairment that that brain's neuro-capacity was insufficient, is uninformative. For it has not been demonstrated that it is the brain's composition that gives consciousness. And that is what must be demonstrated if the insufficiency of brain composition is to be explanatory in the cases of impaired consciousness.

Reasoning, then, in accord with the empirical data suggests that the materialist hypothesis on the nature of consciousness is without the evidence required for truth claims. The hypothesis on the necessity and conditions for unifying sense-data, I have argued, would make consciousness impossible. We saw in the case of our experience of a tree that the findings in our visual percept about the tree's extension in place is confirmed by the sense of touch. We can feel the tree's limbs, trunk, leaves—all of which ground the judgment from vision that "this object is extended." Percepts, i.e., as the tree experience indicates, coincide with that object transmitting the data to sense-faculties. There is a convergence of testimony provided by our awareness outlets to the world.

The data reaching the senses, however, are registered by the sense-receptors as discrete, atomistic, fragmentary electro-inputs—totally dissimilar to the unitary percept that we have when conscious of a tree. For the materialist, for our percepts to be what they are, the data must therefore be unified, synthesized. For he holds it is from these fragmentary material inputs that consciousness, the percept—a unitary whole—arises. Neural activity, however, cannot perform this task. If it is to synthesize the data to resemble the object, it must first have an awareness of what the object looked like in order to synthesize its transmitted data to resemble it. But that awareness, that percept, for the materialist can occur only by first a synthesis of the object's data. And that synthesis itself requires a percept. The end result is a vicious circle: synthesis requires a percept, which percept, though, requires a synthesis in order to become a percept. Awareness could never occur if the materialist hypothesis, as it relates to conditions for resemblance, were correct.

The circle is broken only by granting that the materialist's necessity for unification does not exist, that unification of disaggregated electro-inputs he requires does not occur in the percept's formation. For the percept cannot arise by it. Since, however, the electro-sensory inputs of the brain are disunified, they therefore cannot be the content of the percept. These inputs may be instrumental to the percept's occurrence, intrinsic and necessary to awareness of an object in our world in an immediate and indispensable way. The inputs themselves, however, as disorganized neural-electro quanta cannot be what constitute the percept.

So presenting the materialist requirement of synthesis, we also argued that the electrical charge, electro-event, caused by the interaction of electro-sensory impulses in the brain could not be the percept. Here the condition of resemblance as essential to undermining the materialist hypothesis is not necessary. The thesis can be undermined without it because in the hypothesis that the electrical interaction in an electro-impulse grouping constitutes the percept consciousness is also shown to be impossible. In this case it is not synthesis that is the difficulty with the hypothesis, for in this case synthesis is not invoked. The difficulty, and subsequent impossibility the thesis requires, is how the percept can arise.

We showed that since the impulses received by the brain are numberless, while our percept does not manifest such a condition, either (a) only one impulse grouping could qualify as datum for the percept or (b) the groupings (or impulses), however numberless, were in some way made continuous so that the continuity in our percept could be explained. In the former the selection of the impulse- grouping whose electrical interaction or charge is to be the percept could not be by the electrical interaction itself since then it would have to pre-exist itself. For in the hypothesis it is the effect of those groupings. Nor could electrical interaction provide for a continuity among the impulse-groupings in the brain associated with the percept since all such electrical events in the brain are only momentary. If it is suggested that perhaps a neural filter process blocks all other sensory input groupings from the object to provide the one grouping whose electrical interaction is to be the percept, the resemblance problem can be resurrected in reply. If the percept resembles the object, this filtering must guarantee that the grouping whose electro-interaction resembles the object is not filtered out. But this presupposes awareness of what the object looks like so that the correct grouping be selected. But awareness, if the neural filter suggestion is true, requires the neural filter process, leading once more to a vicious circle.

It is, we should note, this momentariness of electrical impulses which rules out the view that perhaps it is the rapidity with which the object's data strike the sense organ that blocks out their discreteness, their discontinuity. What is in mind here is what movie-projector reels accomplish with frames on a film. Perhaps the speed with which the sense-data strike the sense organ can be likened to that movie- projector effect, providing for the way we experience the data as a whole, a unitary content, rather than as successive and unrelated phases of an object's stimuli.

The electrical impulses resulting from those sense-data would rule out that possibility. They are registered on an electro-encephalogram as discontinuous—abrupt in pulse—and successive. Were the "movie-projector" hypothesis apt, they would instead be registered or recorded as a continuum of stimuli, as uniform, just as the frames of pictures we see in a movie appear as a continuum—not a series of disconnected images. Coherence and steadiness of our percept should be reflected by a uniform continuity in electrical activity—which is precisely the opposite of what is registered on an EEG.

Consciousness, accordingly, does not appear to be reducible to neural electrical activity; nor to be produced by it. Because that activity's electrical charges are material in nature, they cannot constitute the percept. The object's presence in our awareness cannot be reducible, then, to any process of material parts, i.e., the neuro-electrical data resulting from the material stimulus. The impossibilities that arise in asserting the contrary make that clear. Nor, however, can the object enter our awareness as a material whole, as the complete material object. That point is too obvious to argue; the size of the material object is evidence enough to make it. Consciousness, then, does not arise via material parts or material whole. This division, however, comprises all of matter. Therefore, consciousness does not arise materially.

If in examining the neural states and brain mechanisms present in our acts of consciousness we have examined all the states and mechanisms that are in fact present, we need to conclude that consciousness's occurrence must require an immaterial agency. What we have done in our survey of the brain's activity is to examine those neuro-encephalogical factors which are scientifically known to be activated and affected in perception. We then concluded that they could not be causal to consciousness, could not be sufficient to its occurrence. Consciousness cannot be reducible to the brain's electrical activity since the requirements necessary for that reducibility would make consciousness impossible.

The indispensability of our sense-faculties, however, to our awareness of the world makes those faculties a necessary condition for that awareness. The content of consciousness, of our percepts, is information from the world. The sense-faculties are what transmit the data we have of the world, and are thus necessary to our cognitive interaction with that world. A power beyond those neural-sense mechanisms and their electro-disturbances in the brain is required if we are to know what suffices for that interaction. In concert with those mechanisms we have, accordingly, what is both necessary and sufficient for human perception: material input and immaterial agency.

The electro-disturbances of the brain, then, and its specific areas associated with different inputs would be the *material* result of the object's stimuli being received by the sense-neurological apparatus. The percept that results would therefore not be those disturbances.

In what way, then, does the brain relate to awareness? Since we know that excision of certain brain mass inhibits various sense-perceptions, we can reasonably assert that the brain is instrumental in the process of awareness. The data argue for what we have termed the necessary, albeit not sufficient, condition for awareness. The brain is an instrument for cognitive commerce with the world. Its mass serves as a receptor for sense-data received by that body with which the person having the sensations resulting from those data is associated. The brain tissue of my body makes those sensory inputs affecting my body the occasion for *my* consciousness of the world, just as the brain tissue of another individual makes the inputs his body receives the occasion of *his* consciousness of the world.

Exactly what the method of its concert with the immaterial agency to which the data about awareness point is would be, to state the obvious, idle to hypothesize. Squarely facing us is the centuries-worn difficulty of explaining how an immaterial agency can interact with the material world. That there is such interaction, nevertheless, appears to be made manifest when attempting to equate consciousness with material activity. Awareness exists; it cannot be material. Therefore, it must be immaterial. The data give that line of thought palpable reasonability. That we cannot explain the interaction deriving from this line of thought does not invalidate that line of thought.

The Cartesian problem of pinpointing this interaction was answered either by denying the existence of matter in its own right (as in Spinoza) or, for other reasons, altogether (as in Berkeley); or denying the existence of the non-material. The latter, from what we have argued data and evidence show, is without certainty. The former goes against everything our experience tells us.

The material world, we have argued,[19] is made known to us by the presence of surface and resistance. They constitute what is referred to as matter. We may grant that the empty space between electrons on the valence level does not resemble the matter we know, that between sub-atomic bits are empty fields, lacunae. Such lacunae are what chiefly comprise our world, in fact, according to contemporary physics. Our awareness of surface, however, points to the existence of unitary bits that ultimately compose the objects of our world. Surface cannot be empty space or force-fields. Were it the former, all space would appear to us as having surface such that a distinction between the two would never arise for us. It cannot be force-fields, for force-fields have no boundary while surface itself is in fact a boundary. Boundary is what separates, differentiates; and it is unitary "solidities," material bits, that by and through their force-field relationships provide for this boundary and bring to us the awareness of resistance. Their conjunction through the force-fields, physics instructs us, exist at their level grounds our awareness of the world as material. The perception of matter is the perception of surface and resistance that is generated by the relation of material bits in their force-field habitats.

We are on good grounds, then, for advancing the distinction in being between matter and non-matter. On the other hand, difficulty with the epistemology of their interaction however unresolved and opaque, is not good ground for denying that interaction. And we shall not pretend to resolve it here. It has been sufficient simply to establish that the identity of consciousness with material existence is without evidence since our objective has been to amass evidence for man's indestructibility.

That consciousness is not material seems also clear if we look at other acts of consciousness. When we focus on one thing, when we become attentive to it and it alone, is the ignoring of all other stimuli a neural reverberation? Clearly here the one-to-one correspondence hypothesized by some of stimulus with neural occurrence, the neural reverberation, to explain mental activity does not exist. The act of ignoring has no stimulus to which it corresponds. While some thing or event may *cause* it, there is no stimulus that corresponds to intentional disregard. If anything, such disregard is the avoidance of stimuli. If neural events are to be corresponded with stimuli, an act whose very essence is their avoidance appears impossible, as that avoidance, to qualify as a neural event.

What of the experience of understanding a sentence, in distinction from its individual words? While there may be a one-to-one correspondence between brain events and the individual words we read, there is not one between the sentence and brain processes. For we do not read sentences as a unit. We read the words and then have understanding—a residual unit—that is not assignable to any specific word in the sentence. To suggest, in response, that the individual reverberating neural circuits associated with each word in the sentence combine to produce the understanding that comes from the sentence, and that understanding therefore constitutes another neural event, another neural reverberation, requires that the sentence as a unit, a stimulus, first be read so that this circuit's combination, a unit itself, could occur. We do not, however, read sentences this way. Since we do not, and thus there is no brain process that could exist corresponding to our understanding the sentence, a brain processes would not appear to explain how our understanding arises.[20]

We may say the same for the act of comparison. It has no corresponding stimulus in the external world, a fact countering the theory of one-to-one correspondence of brain event with experience in the world. The situation is the same in the experience of expectation. Looking forward into time prescinds one from the present. To deliberately ignore the present, as we do when we *expect*, is not caused by some stimulus that produces "ignoring the present." Rather, it is a deliberate act to turn away from current stimulus. Projecting into the future would likewise be a neural event, on the one-to-one correspondence thesis, as well as the concommitant prescinding from the present that completes the experience of expectation. It is in ignoring present stimuli that we experience this "stepping back" from the present. Establishing a one-to-one correspondence between stepping back and projecting into the future—which are what constitute expectation—with a neural event appears untenable. the stimulus to which stepping back from the present would correspond, that is, ignoring the present, is nowhere to be found. *Why* we would project into the future has no corresponding stimulus either. There are no objects in experience that correspond to "why." Nor is "why" a state produced by neural circuitry. "Why" implies an absence of understanding, but neural states are not associated with absences in awareness. Quite the contrary: one associates a lack of awareness with the absence of a neural state.

The activity of inference further damages the materialist hypothesis. Atomic theory, for example, was first an inference. When originally propounded there was no sense-evidence for the existence of atoms. So also with the heliocentric hypothesis. Countless scientific hypotheses originally unaccompanied by sense-data are similar. Inferential activity, the key to these scientific achievements, is not a product of neural reverberations. To hold that it is to assert that various circuitries in the brain, when firing their electro-chemical products, can generate a new awareness—in this case an awareness that is later confirmed to possess truth—in the absence of the sense stimulus—to cause those firings that the materialist hypothesis holds necessary for this awareness. To make an inference is to conclude to a certain set of data prior to their actual confirming presence. In a one-to-one correspondence theory of stimulus to neural event the presence of those data in the mind prior to confirmatory contact with them is impossible. The contact with their actual existence which is necessary for the one-to-one correspondence has not yet occurred. Nor could the reverberations produce the stimulus to be associated with the inference. They would in such a case be producing that to which they were to conclude, which is impossible. To avoid this impossibility, a conjoining activity that makes explicit the conclusion implied in otherwise disjoined data or premises is needed. That could not be another neural reverberation because there is no stimulus in this case to which that reverberation could correspond.

Consciousness and the material processes of the brain's electro-disturbances show themselves to be different, not identical. Consciousness is other than they. We seem to recognize this in our language. We speak of consciousness as being *of* things; but no material existent is *of* anything in the sense we attribute "of" to consciousness. Consciousness is of a lake; a lake is never "of" a lake. This way of being "of" differs it from material things. They are never "of" themselves in this way or in any other.

Further undermining the materialist thesis is the essential equivalence of the cortical neurons with those in the spine. The former are held to be essential to perception, the latter not. Given their essential equivalence the necessity in the materialist tenet of one to consciousness and not the other presents a difficulty. Why, given the equivalence, one should produce awareness and the other not does not appear explicable physically, since in virtue of their equivalence one would expect them to act in the same way. Similarly there is an equivalence between the spinal synapses and those in the cortex. There is nothing discernible in their molecularity that would indicate why the cortex should be cited as the producer or site of percepts, and not the spinal column. This further substantiates the view that cellular (neural) molecularity does not seem to account for the percept's presence.

The most recent materialist proposition, that computer technology may mirror the brain's operation, is, to put it gently, misplaced. The suggestion that as computer processing is via circuitry and specific "info-chips" so also may the brain's be explained via neural circuitry (neural "chips," if you will) could be anticipated in the variety of neurophysiological models already addressed. We argued that neural electrocircuitry cannot be *causal* in perception: the percept does not arise out of neural-electro disturbances, nor is it those disturbances. A model positing afferent-impulse networking, a variant of those already addressed, gains by this suggestion of network afferences seeming plausibility for the computer/brain comparison. The rhythm of axonal firing and the hierarchy of axonal clusters receiving those firings is hypothesized in the model as a sensory input coding device. Subsequently, it is presumed, the coding of the afferent axon is preserved through all the neural areas receiving the impulse that has now been "coded." And this perhaps explains how sensation occurs in man.

The model appears in Rose's discussion of Mountcastle's experiments on the sense of pressure,[21] and additionally requires a region of "comparator" neurons where the impulse codings are registered. For the model, those codings being registered constitute sensation.

Little seems gained by advancing this axonal apparatus. The required preservation it presumes of the afferent impulse poses the first difficulty. Preservation involves a state transcending the instant, while impulse activity (by which data transmission occurs) is only instantaneous. There is no preservation in the instant; duration, which preservation entails, transcends the instant. This rules out afferent impulse as a possible source of the preservation, a preservation cited as necessary given the nature of human sensation in the model's coding proposal.

The "comparator" cells hypothesized for the registration of the preserved axonal impulse that has worked its way through the neuronal labyrinth can only be of an instantaneous power also. This registration, according to the model, is the sensation. Continued pressure from a stimulus (the subject of Mountcastle's experiments) would require that the sudden nature, the instantaneous existence, of afferent impulses be made continuous so the pressure could be felt the way it is, which is as a continuum. A factor providing for continuity is required because impulses, as we have seen, are not enduring but impermanent. Comparator cells, a the registration site of the stimuli, the cellular network for situating the object's data as sense-information, could not provide this continuity. Their activity, too, can only be sudden—discontinuous and instantaneous—since that is the nature of neuronal activity.

Accordingly, the suggestion of a coding of afferent impulses, whatever might be meant by "coding," would have to ignore the physiological requirements and difficulties we have just noted. In any event, coding as a material or electrical process itself would have to be of the transience characterizing all neuro-electrical events. That is incompatible with the nature of the percept, one of whose features is its constancy. As a suggestion for how percepts are formed, for how sensation occurs,—all the other just noted difficulties notwithstanding—coding of afferent impulses provides no insight, then.

Computers indeed do process their information through a circuitry of electrical impulses and charges via their "info-chips" in a maze of coding that serves man in his resolve for knowledge. The impulses, though, are not percepts: there is no permanence to them; persistence and constancy they do not possess. Brain and computer circuitry may be analogous. Axonal labrynths of dendrites and synaptic transmission may be imaged in computer circuitry and impulse codings. Neither one, though, explain the percept or its occurrence that characterizes human consciousness.

It is clear that "Artificial Intelligence" (AI), is not consciousness. In February, 1990, Dr. Roger Taub of International Business Machines reported that in reproducing a computer (IBM 3090) 10,000 brain cells from the hippocampus brain region the super computer generated waves like those found when recording the brain's electrical waves. This is not surprising. In fact one should expect it if laws of electrical impulses operate universally. From similar conditions similar results should follow. The waves that electrical impulses produce in such circumstances would be similar, and would appear so on an electro-encephalogram. The absence of uniformity in their flow indicates their inability to constitute our percepts, given their uniformity. Additionally the variation of flow suggests a rôle for the cell in this discontinuity of impulse, for one would rightly expect evenness of transmission from the power source used in a computer. Neural cellularity of itself does not provide the required steadiness of electrical charge. The overriding point here, though, is that the impulses registered from the computer replication of hippocampal cells is not evidence that the computer in this case therefore "thought," i.e., duplicated the human act of thinking. To conclude that it did would require the assumption that the brain events registering the wave lines were thoughts. And for this, as already shown, there is no evidence.

Many theorists in the past decade have proposed that possibly computers "think." Such proposals are, however, anthropomorphic. All AI theorists acknowledge that computer operations are effected by algorithms. They can effect their calculations and proofs no other way. If, therefore, we can show that human thought can occur without algorithms we shall have shown that human thought exhibits a feature not possessed by AI. While we may, through the programming of algorithms in a computer, give the computer an ability to process data in an informational way, human intellection and computer processes diverge in their very being if human thought possesses a non-algorithmic feature. Certain human thought processes are obviously algorithmic; most mathematics proceeds as such. Software for computer calculations, since it is designed by man, would be of such algorithmic resolution naturally, when. Human mental processes, however, are not exclusively algorithmic. In showing this, computer processes will be shown not to share in what I have argued human intellection manifests.

It is Roger Penrose[22] who has pointed the argument this way in the example he takes of Gödel's theorem. The reasoning involved requires elaboration of Penrose's comments by certain precisions, as well as additional argumentation that is implied in Penrose's comments and not made explicit by him.

Gödel's theorem conclusively sets forth that not all mathematical truths are demonstrable; more precisely, that at least one is not.[23] While we know that the theorem is true, there can be no algorithm to show that it is. An algorithm is a formula, a method and process of conjoining in thought, mathematical data to arrive at others or at a new datum. Gödel's theorem, however, which we know to be true, is indemonstrable. Its truth is not derivable from equations to which we can point as having led up to or as accounting for it. There is no formula that establishes this indemonstrability in thought, that gives it cogency, or shows its truthfulness.

If the theorem is established, which Gödel has shown it is, without an algorithm, we have a situation of divergence, of dissimilarity, between human thought and artificial intelligence. Gödel's theorem is reached in a way other than is found in artificial intelligence. Since AI occurs only through algorithmic means, arriving at Gödel's theorem is clearly not an instance of it. In the case of Gödel's theorem a truth statement is reached for which AI has no capacity. In their operation and activity human thought and artificial intelligence show themselves to be irreducible to one another: in the instance of Gödel's theorem the evidence is they are different.

We can enlarge upon the argument. Assume Gödel's theorem is false; in other words, that there is no indemonstrable truth. We could only know this by algorithm or insight. In the former that would be by a process of reasoning (series of calculations); in the latter, independently of any such process or steps in thought. Knowledge comes about in other one of two ways: indirectly (as by an algorithm, or series of steps) or directly (this we call insight or intuition). If we know it by the latter, by insight, we are exercising an intellective capacity the computer is known not to have. If by the former, how do we know that algorithm to be true and adequate to disprove Gödel's theorem, to prove, in effect, that there are no indemonstrable truths? If all human thought, like a computer's calculative operations, is by an algorithm, then it is by an algorithm only that we can discern the truth or falsity of any assertion.

If we say it is by an algorithm's practical application, i.e., by the results its usage bring about in actual empirical circumstances in contrast to those in abstract models, that we can discern its truth and adequacy, how do we know that practical application suffices as a criterion? If, in response, we say by an algorithm, we then have to ask how we know that that algorithm is sufficient to defend the usage of practical application as a criterion. By another algorithm? The same problem slides us into an infinite regress. To suggest, on the other hand, self-evidence as the criterion for an algorithm's adequacy as an answer to this conundrum is to admit to an indemonstrable truth; for the self-evident is not demonstrable. The regress, then, can be broken only by granting that some truths are known indemonstrably, i.e., without an algorithm. To assert in the face of all these difficulties that there are still no indemonstrable truths requires for that assertion acceptance of at least one. For since the assertion is not self-evident, it would have to be proven. Proof, though, requires for it a proposition which itself is not susceptible to proof. Otherwise, proof could never begin.

Thus, to disprove or deny Gödel's theorem of the presence of an indemonstrable truth in order to maintain the equivalence of AI with human thought requires accepting as true what one denies. While that does not prove that what is being denied is true, it does prevent the equation of artificial intelligence with human thought. Their identity cannot be shown to be true by its advocates because it cannot be known that there are no indemonstrable truths. Only if it could could the identity of human thought with AI be maintained.

The fact, though, that Gödel's theorem is true directly rules out the equation of AI with human thought. Human thought is not reducible to the computer processing of data.[24] Contained within human intellection is the capacity to see, without need of algorithm, the truth of certain relations or statements. The computer is without that ability; and that differentiates the being of its calculative processes from that of human intellection. Materiality of human thought, therefore, cannot be shown by comparing it to artificial intelligence. The two are not identical.

What emerges from these considerations is the singular lack of evidence for the materialist or reductionist account of human consciousness. In our awareness appears the work of a cognitive agency indisolubly integral to personhood. It is an immaterial power whose communion with the data of the world, via bodily sensory electro-impulses alerting it to objects of that world, gives consciousness its operational and explanatory foundation.

This personhood is the self, whose presence we realize in every conscious event. There is not first a conscious event, and then a process of relating to some entity "the self" to which it is then linked. The conscious event is intimately, simultaneously, of a self in interaction with its world through that body that inextricably completes the reality of human person as agent in this world.

The self, furthermore, can be the object of its own thinking in the activity of self-reflection. The self "looks" at itself in the act of introspection.

It is perhaps an existentialism of sorts to deny that the self could be known to itself, to maintain that introspection is impossible. One fashion holds that the self is not genuinely prehended because the self can never view itself as subject. it is always an object, while equally constitutive of its reality is its being as subject. In self-reflection the self is not really known because in self-reflection it can only be an object to itself, while in its being it is also subject.

In the act of self-reflection, though, I experience myself as subject reflecting upon itself: I know myself as subject. As the one who is reflecting I know it is I who am reflecting, which is precisely what it means to be a subject, that is, to perform an act. That act in these case is that of reflecting. Thus I know myself as subject when I make myself object of my inspection. The self that is knowing is not some being different from the one that is known in this knowing. The self knows itself as subject when it becomes an object of its own knowing. And that cognitive act is one. Otherwise I would not know which being in the introspection was introspecting, while in fact I know that I am that being. Self-reflection is a unity: subject and object are the same.

In this act of introspection an activity inaccessible to material existents emerges. No material existent can be an object to itself. The eye, for example, cannot see itself. The hand cannot grip itself, nor its own gripping. In introspection the self, knowing itself as subject, as that which is introspecting, becomes object to itself as that which is being known, or evaluated, or judged. In this act of self-judgment we have the case of the knower knowing himself as knower.

To so know himself, however, requires that the act of self-reflection be indivisible—not simply undivided. The self, as it were, cannot divide from itself or there would then be two selves: the one knowing, the other known. For then it would not be itself that is knowing, but another, a second, self. This is what I mentioned above: the act of self-awareness must be one. Self-awareness requires that indivisibility be a structure of human personhood, for in self-knowledge what is known is the self that is exercising this knowing, not a second self.

Such indivisibility is absent, however, in material existents. Being formed through the accretion of parts, every material existent is therefore divisible its being; and for that reason, destructible.

The activity of self-awareness, accordingly,, is evidence of an indestructible element in man if it is divisibility that is the only condition for destructibility. Empirically we know that destructibility occurs only through divisibility of an existent. In the next chapter I shall argue that annihilation—an existent without parts ceasing to be—is contradictory. Self-consciousness, then, is neither destructible nor annihilable.

In the case of destruction an existent ceases to be what it was. In annihilation it simply ceases to be. The difference between the two can be shown by this example. The destruction of a tree is not the cessation of being, for the tree becomes another form of being. It becomes humus for the earth. Annihilation is the end of an existent in which the result is nothingness, not another form of being. We have no experience of such an event; it can only be addressed on the level of hypothesis. The closest we can come to picturing it in the case of the tree would be if it were simply to vanish instantly and completely, leaving not a trace of being (wood splinters, wood chips, smoke particulate, humus) behind. Whatever has parts may be destroyed, lose its identity; but in destruction another being comes to be from that which is destroyed.

In annihilation no being remains. If, as I shall argue, annihilation of the self is contradictory, a being whose identity withstands destruction cannot lose its existence by annihilation. It cannot because what is contradictory entails a contradiction, does not take place. Neither annihilation (ending in nothingness) nor destruction of a being through disintegration of parts befalls the self, then. It has no parts, and what is contradictory cannot be happen.

Consciousness, as personally self-reflective, manifests a being that is absent in whatever is only material. At each level of its activity—in perception/sensory awareness, in the act of knowing, and in becoming object to itself—I have suggested in this chapter that the materialist claims about its being either have no foundation or that its activity implies the presence of an entity indistinguishable in its being. In this way the argument from consciousness, man's dominant mode of commerce with the word, is a further argument for personal existence beyond death, for human existence being other than material.

NOTES

1. The case is made most impressively by David Hume, *A Treatise of Human Nature*, Book I, Part IV, Section ii.

2. This methodology of examining an object this way appears in Hume's discussion of causality. "Let us therefore cast our eye on any two objects, which we will call cause and effect, and turn them on all sides, in order to find that impression which produces an idea of such prodigious consequence." *Treatise, op. cit.*, Book I, Part III, Section ii.

3. Paul M. Churchland, *Matter and Consciousness: A Contemporary Introduction to the Philosophy of Mind*, revised ed'n. (Cambridge, MA: M.I.T. Press, 1988). I cite Churchland's well-thought-out presentation as the most comprehensive argument for the materialist position, a position with which he is in sympathy. It is not necessary to respond point-by-point to all his misgivings with the non-materialist outlook to answer his argument. Instead, to answer materialism's hypotheses it is necessary only to point to the impossible consequences to which they lead as well as the gratuitous assumptions materialism makes in presenting its views.

4. In altered states of consciousness, where one's state is more sedate and relaxed, this momentariness of electrical charge does not change. That momentariness of charge is indicated on all EEGs by the angle of descent of any wave. The charge appears to be coming to and end as soon as it occurs. For if the peak in the wave represents the synaptic firing, the descent from that peak makes plain the end of that firing, and the downturn of the charge. What changes, if we look at the EEG of such states, is how often they occur. The time span between them, as indicated by the EEG wavelengths, is greater; for stimuli, as in case of drowsiness (graphed by so-called 0 waves) are not received or registered with the frequency characteristic of the arousal (β wave) state. The change in wave patterns, then, as in between drowsiness and wakefulness, does not mean the electrical firings cause the change in states of awareness—only that stimuli in such states are neurophysiologically registered with differences in their frequency of occurrence. If the awareness level is characterized by the number of stimuli registered, the waking state (when senses are in a ready state, a more stimuli-receptive state) will show *more* wave undulations. That does not indicate that the frequency of synaptic firings, as indicated by the compression of undulations (the distance between each wavelength) that appears on the EEG of one awake constitute our awareness states. The momentariness of such firings rule that out, given the perdurance and constancy that characterize our percepts, our state of awareness.

5. The grid model is a natural enough suggestion for how electrical transmission occurs neurally, given the known ascent of neural complexity travelled by data impulses. The increase in complexity, just as in the increase in the coils of a grid, represent greater charge levels which presumably are achieved as separate electro-impulses begin converging at the levels of increased neural complexity.

6. Karl R.Popper and John C. Eccles, *The Self and its Brain: An Argument For Interaction.* (New York: Springer International, 1977), Part III, p. 534.

7. Daniel Dennet, *Consciousness Explained.* (Boston: Little, Brown, 1991), pp. 268–69.

8. *Ibid.*, Part II, p. 225.

9. J. Z. Young, *Philosophy and the Brain.* (New York: Oxford University Press, 1988), p. 78.

10. *Ibid.*, p. 128, "We might go further and speculate that there may be neurons that represent not only physical objects but words and abstract concepts."

11. *Ibid.*, pp. 125–28.

12. See the quote from Young in note 9, above.

13. Karl R. Popper and John C. Eccles, *The Self and Its Brain, op. cit.*, Part II, p. 314.

14. *Ibid.*, Part II, p. 476.

15. Young has asserted that Libert's findings show simply that "the brain is at work before a subject's conscious intent to act" (p. 73, *Philosophy and the Brain, op. cit.*). The experiment to which he refers in his book, however, is not the one Eccles cites in this instance, which means Young has not addressed the experiment Eccles finds as datum for his position that neural events are not wholly explanatory in awareness. In any event while he did not, his comment that the brain may show neurophysiological changes prior to a conscious decision to act is not laboratory evidence that such changes result in conscious decisions. It is not clear that Young intends for such a conclusion to be drawn. It is also not clear why he would make the comment if that was not the conclusion he wished to be drawn.

16. Daniel Dennet, *Consciousness Explained, op. cit.*, pp. 154–67. Also, Patricia S. Churchland, "The Timing of Sensation: Reply to Libet," *Philosophy of Science*, 48 (1981), pp. 492–97; and Benjamin Libet, "The Experimental Evidence for Subjective Referral of a Sensory Experience Backwards in Time: Reply to P. S. Churchland," *Philosophy of Science*, 48 (1981), pp. 182–97; "Subjective Antedating of the Sensory Experience and Mind-Brain Theories," *Journal of Theoretical Biology*, 114 (1985), pp. 563–70; and "The Timing of a Subjective Experience," *Behavioural and Brain Science* 12 (1989), pp. 183–85.

17. See Robert Lewin, "Is Your Brain Really Necessary?" *Science*, vol. 210 (12 December 1980), pp. 1232–34.

18. D. H. Wilson, A. G. Gazzaniga, and C. Culver, "Cerebral Commisneurotomy for the Control of Intractable Seizures," *Neurology*, 27, pp. 708–15.

19. See note 7, ch. I.

20. These two examples are from Popper, *The Self and Its Brain, op. cit.*, Part I, p. 119. The defense of his example about understanding is mine.

21. Steven Rose, *The Conscious Brain.* (New York: Alfred Knopf, 1973), pp. 100–04.

22. Roger Penrose, *The Emperor's Mind.* (New York: Oxford University Press, 1989). The argument about what the denial of an indemonstrable truth entails, which is presented in the course of the discussion on Gödel's theorem, is mine.

23. Gödel's theorem can be restated as follows: Within an axiomatic system an equation can be constructed such that X=Y, where X states Y cannot be proven. If Y could be proven, what X states is false. But no formal system is such that it permits false propositions to be proved (one cannot prove a false proposition). Therefore, there can be no proof of Y. But this is what Y is asserting, that it cannot be proven. Therefore, Y must be true and true without proof.

24. Some have reduced the debate in this discussion about Gödel's theorem to the question: Could a computer program be written by a computer that was true, but could not be proven by us to be true? If such a program could be written, is this not the same as saying it has proceeded algorithmically? Only if programming can occur without an algorithm at all could this be entertained as a possibility; but a computer cannot begin any program without instructions. The instructions, however, cannot be self-given by the computer, since then the program would never have had a beginning: as self-given, there is no point where the computer could not have already been programming. Since it needs instruction, an algorithm, to begin programming, it cannot reach a non-algorithmic assertion. To do so would be like reaching what cannot be proven through what can be.

V
The Near-Death
Out-of-Body Experience

Since I have required in this book that evidence be the sole arbiter of the claims made for assertions about man's death, the topic of the near-death out-of-body-experience should be examined for its evidentiary quality. Does it say anything conclusive about man's status at the hour of death? Or is it some physiological process having no bearing on the question? Clearly it is a topic more familiar to the populace at large than those treated in the earlier chapters. In a way that is unfortunate, but given the anecdotal quality of near-death accounts it is not to be unexpected. That anecdotal feature, however, does not reduce its importance in an inquiry looking for evidence about man's end. The frequency of reports of the near-death account among the population merits for it the exercise and attention of analysis. Where a sufficient number believe something is true or has happened, impartiality requires that their case be heard.

The empirical studies of near-death researchers in the last two decades—e.g., Moody, Ring, and Sabom[1]—accord with the emphasis on evidence that objectivity presumes. With Ring especially the marked role of evidence as unconditional for any immortality discussion sharply predominates. All three researchers begin with a weight, an anchor, of *in situ* actual experiences in the near-death circumstance. Important in this whole effort is the verifiability and repetition of their findings, two absolute requirements of scientific method. Their procedure for inquiring whether anything deathless is reliably registrable is pronouncedly empirical. And that has made for the wide-ranging interest the subject has received today.

The reason for the near-death research of the past ten years becomes plain when we examine the claim of so many who have been "near death." Near-death experiences (NDEs) correlate very heavily with what has been described as heavenly, paradisaical, transcendent. Those who have had an NDE have spoken, in compelling numbers, of what they assert can only be termed non-worldly, but yet very real and in no way hallucinatory. For them the phenomenon is a real human experience, a genuine—as opposed to imagined—event. Indeed, the frequent feeling of passivity in the NDE, as related by those who have had it, would argue against a subjective initiation of the event, suggesting the need for a more careful explanation.[2] The individual's affirmation of it as an experienced reality brings it to the concrete.

Departure from the shores of our previous chapters begins, then, with a brief review of the empirical data, solid witness, recorded by the academicians of the near-death phenomenon. Concommitant with improved medical techniques at resuscitation and life extension in the 1960s and so on, beneficiaries of such techniques in increasing numbers began to report experiences in their life trauma that are not experienced in any other life situation.[3] So unlike is this experience from any other that some reporting it have described it as inexpressible. At the crisis of near-death, where the coronary victim has suffered from the failed heart, the suicide attempt been almost successful, the accident victim returned from the edge of death, arises a constellation of moments that whispers of a supernal country. " . . . a feeling of easeful peace and a sense of well-being . . . a sense of overwhelming joy and happiness. This ecstatic tone . . . tends to persist as a constant emotional ground as other features of the experience begin to unfold. At this point, the person is aware that he feels no pain nor does he have any other bodily sensations . . . These cues suggest to him that he is either in the process of dying or has already 'died'.

> He may then be aware of a transitory buzzing or a windlike sound . . . he finds himself looking down on his physical body, as though he were viewing it from some external vantage point . . . aware of the actions and conversations taking place in the physical environment" (as) "a passive, detached spectator. All this seems very real—even quite natural to him; it does not seem at all like a dream or an hallucination.
>
> At some point he may find himself in a state of dual awareness . . . aware of 'another reality' and feel himself being drawn into it . . . the experience here is predominantly peaceful and serene.
>
> The presence . . . stimulates him to review his life and asks him to decide whether he wants to live or die . . . he has no awareness of space

and time. Neither is he any longer identified with his body. Only the mind is present.

Sometimes, however, the decisional crisis occurs later or is altogether absent, and the individual undergoes further experiences. He may, for example, continue to float through the dark void toward a magnetic brilliant golden light, from which emanates a feeling of love, warmth, and total acceptance. Or he may enter into a 'world of light' and preternatural beauty, to be (temporarily) reunited with deceased loved ones before being told, in effect, that it is not yet his time and that he has to return to life.[4]

This is the being of the full NDE. In *Heading Towards Omega* Kenneth Ring, to quote him again, has neatly delineated the features of this "core NDE." " . . . there is no time in these experiences ('It was eternity' . . . 'It's like I was always there and I will always be there . . . '), there is a certain feeling of progression.

. . . we remember (1) the incredible speed and sense of acceleration as one approaches (2) the light that (3) glows with an overwhelming brilliance and yet (4) does not hurt one's eyes . . . one feels in the presence of light (5) pure love, (6) total acceptance, (7) forgiving of sins, and (8) a sense of homecoming; that (9) communication with the light is instantaneous and nonverbal and that the light (10) imparts knowledge of a universal nature as well as (11) enables one to see or understand his entire life so that (12) it is clear what truly matters in life . . . one may be aware of (13) transcendental music, (14) paradisiacal environments, and (15) cities of light as one progresses further into the experience . . . finally (16) once having encountered the light, one yearns to be with it forever.[5]

The strength of this report of near-death experience is the experience's widespread occurrence, in part or whole, among the living that have been declared dead and been revived. Its breadth, according to a Gallup poll, amounts to a 35% occurrence, conservatively, among the NDErs. That numbers in the millions.[6]

The possibilities here of prevarication, mass suggestion, and wish-fulfillment have been minutely examined, and convincingly dismissed. Drug inducement of the NDE has been cogently ruled out with alert reasoning power by Kenneth Ring. Carol Zaleski, in analysis published after Ring, likewise concluded that the pharmacological explanation is not conclusive.[7] No physiological explanation of the event consistent with the event has been successfully tendered. Neurophysiological studies have yet to show that the near-death experience is, or might be, strictly a bodily defense mechanism, the brain's chemically fashioned weapon against the final test. Kenneth Ring's *Life At Death* has enlighteningly addressed that difficulty: the current state of knowledge does not trace this reaction to the unknown to a programmed neurophysiological response.[8]

Instead, those who have had an NDE have held it to be of the same texture and presence as ordinary experience. That is what has compelled their insistence on the NDE as non-illusory, non-hallucinatory. Psychiatric review of the NDE has shown it incompatible with mental disorder. Psychoses are cut from different cloth. A near-death experience is neither mental illness nor a symptom of it.[9]

But those who have had an NDE that they reported did not die in it. Lazarus died. His story has been told elsewhere, unaccompanied by an NDE narrative. He had been entombed. And in our day *rigor mortis* is still the sure sign that embalming may begin. No individual who has reported an NDE cited in the research has undergone *rigor mortis* in the NDE. Kastenbaum has elaborated how it is that the NDE, on these grounds, does not move us one step closer to demonstrating the immortality thesis.[10]

He may have drawn this conclusion too quickly, given the frequently reported out-of-body experience (OBE) in the NDE. This particular facet of the near-death event his study does not treat. In contrast to the simple near-death experience, i.e., one unaccompanied by this OBE, might the OBE in the near-death trauma present tolerable evidence for an actual demarcation from the body by the one undergoing the near-death OBE? Is there in it ground for asserting a sure separation from matter, a positive delineation from corporeal limits, for the one who has had this OBE? If so, evidence of an incorporeal reality for man is suggested.[11]

In its most basic meaning an out-of-body experience is a personal consciousness and activity accomplished without the body. The human person in the OBE realizes, in addition, that he is out of the body. He is certain that the body which he has always had in life, and through which he has been present in the world as a living being, is wholly separated from his out-of-body state. He is existing as a self continuous with his past, with the powerful exception that his selfhood, his existence, is not bodily. His identity is intact, and he knows this to be so. His material body, however, is not a constituent of that identity which he knows to be his, and which identity he knows in his OBE to be non-bodily. His human being is not bodily being. His existence as a self as "left the body behind." There has been a separation of consciousness from matter.

The description of the near-death OBE by those who have had it points to this separation. " . . . 'a real floating sensation. . . . It seemed like I was up there in space and just my mind was active. No body feeling. . . . Weightless, I had nothing. . . . I was above. I don't know above what . . . like I didn't have a body . . . but it was not me. Not a body, but me. . . . The real me was up there, not this here' (pointing to her physical body)."[12]

" . . . 'I was walking away from myself hanging there'," is how a suicide attempt described his OBE. Another, " . . . 'I felt I had left my body and I had viewed it from the other side of the room . . . looking back at myself. . . . I can remember seeing myself up there with a sheet and a hypothermia blanket on me.'" "'I was up in the lefthand corner of the room, looking down at what was going on.'"[13]

From others, " . . . 'I was just observing . . . It'" (the resuscitation procedure) "'didn't feel as though it was happening to me at all. I was just the observer'." "'I was totally objective . . . just an onlooker.'"[14]

In Ring's *Life At Death* sampling, 37% underwent a near-death OBE. But any value they would have as evidence for us of non-bodily awareness—of consciousness as immaterial—would require that the OBE reports of events prehended out of body be accurate. In the situation above of the hospital OBE patients, e.g., what they recounted would have to square with the events that those attending these patients could confirm as actually having happened. In a comatose state—the near-death condition—the senses are shut down. These are our channels of awareness of the world. Bodily embedded, they are our source of information about our environment and surroundings. In the absence of any one of them our awareness in some way becomes restricted. In the total absence of operating, working, sense-faculties we are shut off from the world.

In the near-death state sensory capability has ceased. No one in this state is conscious externally, because sense transmission has stopped. Physiologically, sensation has become incapacitated. Its integrity, which consists in the sense organ's vital interaction with various brain centers, has been impeded. In trauma, either part or all of the bodily sensory-neural-brain network has been injured or shut down. If sensation is our only avenue of awareness of the world, and is only bodily, awareness of the world in the absence of sensory powers would indicate non-bodily awareness.

The meaning from this: if human awareness is not only bodily, occurs independently of the body, being a conscious individual is not being only a bodily one. Human individuality and human body would not be the same, then. Corruption of the human body, accordingly, need not be corruption of the human individual.

To test the accuracy of the near-death OBE reports, reports held to be based on awareness of events in the absence of bodily sense transmission, Michael Sabom undertook a methodological inquiry into their veracity. If an unconscious near-death trauma victim claiming an OBE gave an account of his crisis treatment and surroundings derivable only from bodily sense operations, his claim to being out of the body could not be lightly dismissed. To have an awareness of events in the absence of sensation is to have it without the body. The only routes for awareness are the sensory pathways. And they need a functioning body, one whose sense-faculties (sensory-neural receptors) are operant to carry out their work of data transmission. Sabom's *Recollection of Death*[15] is his scientific study of the phenomenon testing for inconsistencies in and improbabilities of the accuracy of patient resuscitation OBE reports. He pinpointed six representative OBE testimonials and corroborated them with the accounts of the medical team involved in the resuscitation with cross-reference to the patient's clinical records. Only transbodily capabilities, i.e., an actual OBE, could account, Sabom reasoned, for the accuracy of the patient's description of the clinical events surrounding revival. That is because an unconscious body cannot have the awareness indicated to be present in these OBE reports.

A patient declared clinically moribund would recount events, after medical restoration, in the resuscitation procedure inaccessible to one's threshold in the comatose state. Verification of these events, e.g., the peculiarity of a medical procedure, identification of individuals in that procedure, or the steps taken at the trauma center, would take place through testimony of the medical personnel involved. Actual hospital records and post-resuscitation/operation data acted as a double-check on the reported OBE. For Sabom, the contention that there was an OBE was well-nigh authenticated, as his documentation argues.

What of Sabom's methodology? Is it exhaustive? Does it exclude all room for error? Are those certifying the accuracy of the OBE reports being less than candid? They have no reason to be, for nothing would be gained. And in light of the common scepticism in response to the unusual, the risk of those interviewed losing respectability would be great. While that is not indisputable confirmation of candor in the OBE verification by hospital personnel, it is perhaps the strongest that the cases allow. And that is all that can be asked in instances where evidence—absolute indisputability—is impossible of attainment. The level of indisputability the testimony of hospital personnel has here depends on how much strength we attribute to the motive against loss of respectability.[16]

Was Sabom's method exhaustive? Is there some significant variable it failed to address? It does not appear so. In seeking to verify OBE accounts he has consulted all those who could verify them, and gone a step further through his cross-reference double-check.

Does the methodology exclude all room for error? Error (as distinct from falsehood) could result from incompetence, lack of understanding, or faulty information.[17] None of the principals involved have suggested, after Sabom's interviews were published, that he was misinformed. And we have no evidence of incompetence. He has executed his research within the normal rigors of academic inquiry. That separates it from a merely anecdotal summary. If there is, then, any incompetence in *Recollections* it would have to be in the methodology of scientific inquiry itself. That would be a novel criticism, and not well-based. And nowhere in his deliberations has Sabom, a medical doctor, shown a failure to comprehend the data amassed, or their implications.

The Sabom data, accordingly, allow for a compelling case about non-bodily awareness. In terms used in law courts might we have what is called "the preponderance of the evidence"? Witnesses certifying the accuracy of a near-death victim's OBE reports have come forth. Their testimony has been checked against other data for the sake of reverification. Lying has been ruled out, as far as circumstances allow. And no circumstances point to a compelling benefit to lie: motive has been eliminated. Denying the validity of OBE reports is, then, to deny the preponderance of at least the data, if not the evidence.

Assuring the veridicality of the OBE rests on the testimony of witnesses and objective records. For this reason a strong case can be made for Sabom's results. *If* non-sensory awareness is a bodily impossibility, then those who claimed that their awareness of clinical events, whose accuracy was verified, was in fact out of the body have spoken truthfully.[18]

The OBE in this situation transcends those arguments levelled against the near-death experience that does not contain it. While it could be argued that natural endorphins or drugs induced the feelings and visions reported in the NDE—even though there is no evidence for that claim—the veridicality of the OBE renders those arguments pointless. They have nothing to do with the circumstances of veridicality. In the OBE there is no "vision" for which to account. In the OBE it is the actual awareness of a comatose body that must be explained. We are faced with circumstances in which the bodily apparatus of sensory data-reception has ceased to function while the individual whose body has so ceased has nevertheless verified awareness of his surroundings.

There is some suspicion that the auditory apparatus may still have capability in the comatose body, a suspicion for which there is no neurophysiological evidence. Even granting that capability, the visual accuracy exhibited in the veridicality of the OBE, in which the patient sees what is being done in the trauma setting, is inexplicable in bodily terms. The eyes are shut. If endorphins or drugs provide for trans-sensate awareness—out-of-body veridicality—how they provide sight in this instance becomes problematic. In this way the point can be made: The materialist paradigm is inapplicable here. Awareness has become, apparently, non-bodily. How else does one account for seeing when the bodily faculty by which one sees is not in use? That is the issue, root and branch, in the out-of-body report at near-death. Until it is resolved the materialist doctrine that awareness can only be bodily appears once more as inconclusive.

If the out-of-body experience does exist, the experience itself could not be bodily. This can be shown in both the order of thought and in that of actual existence. In the former, where it is just the notions involved, and thus without reference to an actual situation, the body cannot be conceived as separate from, outside of, itself, as that which, in the OBE separates from itself. Separated from body it would cease to be the body that separated, for body separate from itself would be body other than itself. Body separate from itself, as that which in the OBE was "out of" itself, involves necessarily the element of distinction. To conceive of the body as distinct from itself involves two mental objects: that of the body, and of the very same body separate from itself. In such a case we are thinking of two identical bodies as distinct from each other. Approached from the order of thought, then, analysis shows that the out-of-body experience cannot be the experience of a body.

In the order of being (as opposed to the order of thought) a body *actually* distinct and separate from itself requires two existent bodies—the body and, in addition, the body from which it is distinct. But they are the same bodies: they must be to be the body of the person having the OBE. If not, we are left with two bodies different from each other, and inhabited by a conscious-ness that is (a) in the two bodies at once, (b) in the out-of-body body alone, or a situation in which (c) there are two minds in two bodies or (d) a mind in the comatose body and not the OBE body. One mind in two bodies for the same person seems incon-ceivable. How would it be present in them? Not by parts;the mind is not a magnitude. A mind in the out-of-body body instead of the comatose one would mean the coming-to-be of a mind in that body, or a mind that left the comatose one to enter the out-of-body one. In the first, how did the mind come to be in it? In the second, how did it leave the comatose one? Two minds in two bodies involve difficulties similar to those just mentioned. And what happens to the second mind, which is necessary for awareness, in the out-of-body body, i.e., the body other than the comatose one, when the OBE ends? And a mind in the comatose body, but not the OBE one, would fail to explain awareness in the comatose one whose senses were not functioning, for it is senses that are the routes of awareness of and from the world. It is this comatose body, by hypothesis, which must account for the OBE awareness, since the mind, without which there is no awareness, is in our hypothesis now only in this body, and not the OBE one. The assertion of two bodies in an OBE, consequently, appears without strength. The out-of-body experience, then, as addressed in terms of the order of being, has cause, in the same way we saw in the argument from the order of thought, for being viewed as non-bodily.

The point is important, for we are seeking to ascertain if there is a non-bodily, a non-material, dimension in man. If the OBE excludes a body, which we have just argued it does, then we have the evidence of incorporeality that we need—if there are experi-ences out of the body. The grounds for excluding a second body, and thus the body altogether, in the OBEs appear well-founded, if the reasoning process we just went through has the appropriate rigor. In the OBEs the awareness must be non-bodily, non-corporeal. If there is an experience actually out of the body, consciousness is not bodily-constrained.

The point in bringing up the out-of-body near-death experience should be plain, then. In the current state of science it has no explanation. To label it hallucinatory, of course, is to misuse the adjective. Hallucinations have no veridicality. And it is that veridicality that requires a cause. How can one have awareness if it must be bodily-derived and the senses, bodily composed, are inoperant? All experience runs contrary to insensate awareness. Unarguably, in a healthy state awareness is always sense-driven. We have argued that some immaterial capacity is requisite if sense transmission is to result in a percept, a conscious event. Here, however, in the OBE the necessity of sense origination seems to be overridden.

Limiting ourselves, as we should, to what the data allow us to conclude, permits this reading of the OBE: Either awareness can be bodily-originated in the absence of sense-faculties, or awareness does not, as a *sine qua non*, require the body, which it nevertheless does when one is functioning normally. There may be instances, i.e., in which communion with the body is suspended, breached, and consciousness takes on an existence of its own disjoined from the body. The alternative is equally problematic: awareness can require a body, but the sense powers are not what always generate it. The only evidence we have of this is the OBE, which can be equally interpreted as evidence that consciousness can be non-bodily, that it does not *require* a body. This equality of interpretability of one and the same event becomes a difficulty for the materialist view of man. What it has asserted cannot be the case, that is, non-bodily or non-sensory originated awareness appears, given the OBE's veridicality, equiprobable with what it has asserted must be the case, that is, the functioning of a healthy body in each case of awareness. Quite plainly this reduces the materialist tenet to the level of opinion; which requires, for its passage to that of truth, evidence that it cannot provide.

Given that, the OBE is not explicable in terms of sensory powers. Accordingly, asserting a bodily, and therefore material, necessity, to awareness on the premise that human awareness requires man's sensory apparatus will leave unexplained an awareness capability that does not reduce to the materialist model. This is to say awareness has no determining materialistic explanation—which it needs if man is to be explained in terms of matter.

The topic of the out-of-body experience provides occasion to revisit the subject of the incorporeal that occupied us in the second chapter. We have argued that an incorporeal aspect in man means an incorruptible one. Partibility, the precondition for decay, is absent in the immaterial. And evanescence, where in the absence of parts there is a gradual, and ultimately total, loss of existence has not been demonstrated, as we argued in that chapter against Kant.

It remains to consider annihilation,[19] a sudden, instantaneous end to human immateriality, an end to its existence not occurring evanescently or through break-up of parts. Can an existent not susceptible to termination through parts, that is, the immaterial, be annihilated? Can it cease existing such that its end, unlike the case of destruction, is not a changeover to another existence or form of being, but simply to nothingness?

One difficulty in such a hypothesis is to picture to oneself a changeover to nothingness. It is unimaginable. Our experience of change is always that that which changes changes into something else, even if that change means the end of existence for the thing that is changing. We cannot make intelligible to ourselves a changeover to nothing. Strictly speaking, furthermore, a changover to nothing means that there has been no changeover.

This difficulty aside, allow as conceivable an end to an immaterial existent such that its end results in its becoming, its being, nothing. Its annihilation would require an agency other than itself, an external cause capable of annihilating it: Nothing can annihilate itself, since in that case it would be more powerful than itself. That such an external agency exists is not demonstrable; nor is there evidence of such.

And one argument against it can be proposed. It is exceptional such an external agency, such a malevolent existent, capable of annihilating man in his being would not annihilate— or prevent—human existence from the first. Were human existence malevolent, a malevolent agency would not terminate it since its goal would be malevolence. Human existence as malevolent, though, does not appear to be a sustainable claim. If human existence is a good, i.e., something preferable to non-existence, a malevolent agent, it would seem by definition, would seek to prevent such a good, human existence, from the first. Thus nothing human would exist. Allowing some existence to man, rather than none, would be a contradictory act, therefore, for a malevolent being. Further, if man is immaterial in some way and it is only, in our hypothesis of malevolent agency, after death that a malevolent agent would end man's immaterial existence, the purpose of man's immateriality, i.e., survival of bodily decomposition, would be unintelligible. What is gained by his possession of immateriality if bodily decomposition could have been the instrument for his termination?

If man is immaterial in any way, he is so in his being. He does not become immaterial at some stage of his existence. If he is immaterial, he is so by his very humanity. As a result, since it is contradictory for a malevolent agent not to prevent existence, existence (in virtue of its preferability to non-existence) being a good, for man to have existence for a certain period, or at all, would be a contradictory act for a malevolent being. Even for that malevolent being to exist would be a contradiction because existence is a good, and thus an impossibility in the intrinsically malevolent. Given this contradictoriness of malevolent agency (the contradictoriness being that {a} by the very fact of its malevolence existence for it should be impossible and {b} that untold numbers of humans have existed, which is incompatible with malevolence since its very requisite is non-existence), those asserting a malevolent agent in wait to end man's immaterial existence would have to account for this two-fold contradictoriness. They would have to show how such malevolence, in spite of the contradiction its existence would involve, could nevertheless exist. They would also have to show how man could exist, given the incompatibility that has with malevolence.

We can, then, with some assurance rule out the existence of this malevolent agent and allow as reasonable the proposition that immaterial existence is inextinguishable. It cannot be annihilated. While bodily identity is lost in decomposition, immaterial existence, not being decomposable or annihilatable, retains its identity in virtue of its immateriality. Human selfhood, for whose incorporeality we argued in chapter 4, would therefore retain its identity in the body's decomposition. What was ingredient to the self in life, viz., bodily integration, is not to its immateriality. We come back to the point made in chapter 1: human life and human existence are not the same. Life is a phase of that existence—the bodily phase. It is not the whole of it.

NOTES

1. The results of recent research into death and dying are well-known and broadly publicized in this country. Among the recent best presentations are Raymond Moody, *The Light Beyond* (New York: Bantam, 1988); Melvin Morse, *Closer To the Light* (New York: Villard, 1990); Kenneth Ring, *Heading Towards Omega* (New York: William Morrow, 1984) and *Life At Death: A Scientific Investigation of the Near-Death Experience* (New York: Coward, McCann, and Geoghehan, 1980); Michael Sabom, *Recollections of Death* (New York: Harper and Row, 1982); and Carol Zaleski, *Otherworld Journeys: Accounts of Near-Death Experience in Medieval and Modern Times* (New York: Oxford University Press, 1987). A sceptical view of the near-death experience as evidence for survivability by an advocate of survival as a reality is Robert Kastenbaum's *Is There Life After Death?* (New York: Prentice-Hall, 1984).

2. The reported feelings of transport and, upon return to human bodily awareness, of being pulled into the body indicate this passivity.

3. While in fact there are various ethereal experiences not associated with the near-death crisis, Moody details their difference from the near-death circumstance (see Moody, *op. cit.*). One such type of experience unrelated to the NDE is elaborated in Robert A. Monroe, *Far Journeys* (Garden City: Doubleday, 1987) and *Journey Out of the Body* (Garden City: Doubleday, 1977), *passim.* I am not especially enlightened by Monroe's work.

4. Kenneth Ring, *Life at Death, op. cit.*, pp. 102–03.

5. Kenneth Ring, *Heading Towards Omega, op. cit.*, p. 83.

6. *Ibid.*, pp. 34–34. Also, George Gallup, with William Proctor, *Adventures in Immortality* (New York: McGraw-Hill, 1982).

7. Zaleski does not hold that therefore the NDE is evidence of immortality—simply, that explaining the NDE by drugs does not advance our knowledge of the NDE's cause. Ring has not claimed for the NDE the status of evidence for immortality. He has suggested that the denial of immortality is certainly not helped by the NDE phenomenon.

8. Kenneth Ring, *Life at Death, op. cit.*, pp. 215–17.

9. See Raymond Moody, *The Light Beyond, op. cit.*, pp. 85–94.

10. See Robert Kastenbaum, *Is There Life After Death?, op. cit.*, pp. 39–40. Kastenbaum, in contrast to Zaleski, is far too quick with his assertion that the NDE is "an adaptive psychobiological function"—a defense mechanism in the face of death. The evidence is far from certain, as Carol Zaleski, (*op. cit.*, pp. 168–83) amply points out.

11. The near-death OBE is quite specific of evidence, not to be associated with autoscopic hallucinations. The important differences between the two appear in Moody, *op. cit.*, pp. 97–98.

12. Kenneth Ring, *Life At Death, op. cit.*, pp. 45–46.

13. *Ibid.*, p. 46.

14. *Ibid.*, p. 49.

15. See note 1.

16. Only faulty memory or recall of the OBE-reported medical/clinical details could be the other cause of the inaccuracy. Sabom's clinical records cross-check furnishes a useful buffer in this regard. The records in question were drawn up quite shortly after the OBE event(s), minimizing the possible effects of the passage of time.

17. The last two differ in that lack of understanding could still occur despite correct information, while faulty information could never produce understanding.

18. I rule out telepathy as a means of awareness. Telepathy, if it does occur, is not associated with traumatized states. Also, it is always accompanied, according to those who believe in or report it, by sentiments that are vague, indefinable—descriptions not fitting the reported near-death OBE. Those having experienced it characterize it as a state of acuity. A readable intelligent study of telepathy and the like as it relates to survivability as David Lorimer's *Survival? Body, Mind, and Death in the Light of Psychic Experience* (London: Routledge and Kegan Paul, 1984). Notwithstanding Lorimer's erudite presentation, I remain to be convinced of telepathic capabilities.

19. The notion of annihilation appears in Aquinas's *Summa Theologiae*, I, Question LXXV, art. 7, reply to objection 2. Annihilation appears to mean a sudden termination, instantaneous reduction to non-being, to nothingness—the very opposite of creation, the bringing to be out of nothing. We have no experience of annihilation (or creation), for which reason I am not certain of the force a discussion on it has or could suggest.

VI
Other Theories.
And Questions.

In this book evidence has been the criterion for drawing conclusions about man's status in death. It has been the measure
of their validity. Pointing that out does not belabor the obvious,
that this is the role expected of evidence. Evidence, as we have
seen has not been the test for a variety of pronouncements about
man's being. Evidence is what brings inquiry to an end such that
with it inquiry has no further to proceed with respect to what
provoked the inquiry. That about which we inquired, when
evidence has been reached, is answered. Assertions and positions
that can be overturned do not possess, then, the character of
evidence. That is the case with the assertions and positions of the
materialist.

There are two remaining hypotheses about human death to
consider. They merit the same criterion that has been applied so
far. They are (1) reincarnation and (2) parapsychological testimony claimed for *post mortem* survival.

(1) Reincarnation is, of course, the doctrine that each of us
has lived before, and that our present life—all its circumstances
and conditions—is the result of one's previous lives. Our world
today is a consequence of how we have all acted in previous lives.
Our world tomorrow will be caused by how we all live in this. Individually, reincarnation is meant to explain why I am the way I
am today, why I was born with certain capabilities and not others,
why inequalities in riches and circumstances exist, and why
certain things attract me and others do not. The explanation is to
be found in how I have acted in my prior lives. Reincarnation is a
cycle of cause and effect expressing a universal law of compensa-
tion: My life today is reward or punishment for lives gone by.
Whatever I am today is the harvest from seeds I planted in the

furrows of another life. Tomorrow's harvest is being planted today. How others have lived in the past forms the world today in which they and I now live. How they live today forms the world in which I shall live tomorrow.

It is a difficulty to delineate precisely the moral or "kharmic" component in the doctrine from its other features. It is sufficiently large, and is perhaps what accounts for the teaching in the first place. There is an eternal over self (atman). An empirical (manifest) self imposed in successive bodily rebirths constitutes the process of lives as the individual must learn and achieve self-betterment. Each empirical self comprises another stage separate from all prior stages in the development of the permanent self. Kharma requires that this self be eternal: Bodily death is always a transition stage for re-entry into another body until perfection comes. In Western terms, the personality never dies; only the body does.

Empirical attempts to verify actual past lives are well-known. None have been conclusive. Anecdotal reports of accurate familiarity with events and places existing prior to one's birth have been explained by possible causes that do not require an actual prior bodily existence.

Do these explanations have validity? One such is that individuals through telepathic accessing of a "universal unconscious" can relate events at which they could not have been physically present. This may account, it is suggested, for how they know things from a "past world." While we have no evidence of this universal source, we have none of a prior life either. In science the procedure seems to be to avoid what is unfamiliar when something more familiar may do. On these grounds, favoring a "universal unconscious" that is telepathically tapped seems less of a difficulty than believing in actually having lived before. This is so because we seem to have familiarity with something akin to this unconscious in our sleeping. This cannot be said of a prior life, however. It carries with it nothing of the familiar. Regarding reincarnation, there is also Tertullian's objections that reincarnation implies a fixed number of souls, but the world's population is steadily increasing, as well as that of bodily continuance—i.e., why would an aged man, in his reincarnation, reappear in a child's body with a child's behavior and not his own? Also there is the question of where these souls go in the time between incarnations.

Telepathy, non-verbal communication at a distance, is also familiar. Anecdotally, an evidentiary case of sorts can at least appear possible. In a phrase from everyday speech, "it is something to which we can relate." A prior existence, it seems clear, cannot be so characterized. It does not have the features that enable us to view something as, if not implausible, at least plausible.

And if we look at what the doctrine of reincarnation is meant to explain, problems with it surface that appear persuasive against an actual prior life for any individual. While the lack of evidence for pre-existence made it, in our characterization, something unfamiliar, the problems encountered in what it is meant to explain appear to make it simply untenable.

Reincarnation postulates endless past lives that explain our current life—its material circumstances, conditions, and how we treat others and are treated by them. An endless number of past lives cannot explain a current life, however. Each life requires a prior life for its explanation when there is an endless number of them purported to explain this one. Nothing is explained then; before you can explain any one life, a prior life has to be explained. In this setting, reincarnation fails.

If, on the other hand, we postulate a first life and innumerable subsequent ones, we still are left with explaining the conditions that beset the first life. Reincarnation cannot explain it, for the first life is not a reincarnation. That is true by the very meaning of "first life." Consequently, reincarnation cannot explain our current state, this life. If reincarnation is meant to explain each life, it cannot explain lives subsequent to a first life, since there is no first life for it to explain. And where there is no first, there is no subsequent: In any series, that to which something is subsequent is first in relation to it. There could be no second or subsequent were there not this "first." In the situation in which the lives are finite in number reincarnation cannot be an explanation of any of them.

Neither an endless nor finite number of past lives, then, tells us why some were born into wealth, others abject poverty, why some grew to be beautiful or handsome, others not. What is required for reincarnation, accordingly, that is, the existence of deathless self, is no longer required since what reincarnation was meant to explain it does not. As a teaching for individual immortality, reincarnation must be rejected. Its value for instruction lies elsewhere.[1]

(2) The paranormal communication with the dead has also been advanced as an indication that man is immortal. Information gained in paranormal settings has been said to be possible only if the dead have actually communicated with the living. Coincidence as an explanation is ruled out on the grounds that acquisition of correct information is too frequent, while what happens by coincidence is rare. There are too many documented cases of such acquisition to attribute them to happenstance, and too many assumptions of dubious worth that are advanced to account for how this information is attained. The more the number of dubious assumptions required to explain this acquisition, it is argued, the less credible they appear as an explanation. Taken together, the argument continues, it is easier to believe the dead communicated the information in question than the assumptions advanced on the grounds that the dead could not have.

There does not appear at this time to be any way either to prove or to disprove the arguments for or against the paranormal. Arguments from improbability seem persuasive against it, but leave too much unexplained to be conclusive. On the other hand, belief that information could have come in any way other than from communication with the dead seems too large a step to take. How we come to know things, i.e., what the capacity of the mind is, is far from understood. Hunches, e.g., are borne out. Premonitions are vouched for as having been expressed by an individual before the event about which the premonition was expressed occurred.

How both can be seems inexplicable. Learning of things that seem impossible to explain given our current understanding of man's powers of mind might not appear impossible as (and if) the mind's capacity becomes further understood. Centuries may pass till that time; but it is better to wait centuries and be right than be wrong by not waiting at all. We may find that our mental powers while we are living are adequate to what we thought only messages from the dead could explain.

What does appear certain is the invalidity of the materialist account of mind. The brain does not explain consciousness. The result of that certainty presents us, it will be objected, with a dualism. How can an immaterial agency interact with a material organ?

If it were impossible, we would be left with the same difficulties that we showed materialism to possess. The impossibility of such interaction, however, cannot be demonstrated. One cannot point, furthermore, to a piece of evidence which certifies the impossibility of dualist interaction. Nor is there any feature about the immaterial that makes its causality with material being impossible. Its non-spatiality does not eliminate *a priori* its ability to work within space; for it cannot be proven that space can only interact with other spatially existent beings. Nor can it be demonstrated that causality can occur only among beings that possess material extension. There are, accordingly, neither inductive nor deductive grounds for dismissal of immaterial causality in a being that has materiality, or is material. There is nothing inherently impossible about such interaction. Were there, it seems improbable that we could have shown the impossibilities the materialist account of mind evidently entails.

The distinction between a material body and immaterial human power suggests, additionally, the presence of two distinct beings in man. The objection conceives of immaterial and material being, then, as two *things* that need to be conjoined. How immateriality and materiality come into contact is one difficulty that follows from this manner of conceiving. We think of causality as being by contact, as in the case of billiard balls striking each other. In the case of contact we are able to trace an action or movement to something antecedent. What sort of antecedence immateriality possesses in this context seems elusive. Thus is ruled out immaterial efficacy in the world.

There is nothing about causality, though, that requires its occurrence be by the contact of one thing with another. Certainly premises of a syllogism are neither things nor continuous (spatially adjoining); i.e., they are not in contact. Yet we say premises cause a conclusion.[2]

Clearly it is not the constraints of some theoretical framework, some limitation of how we use words, that explains how we come to talk dualistically about man, i.e., to talk about *a* mind and *a* body. It is our current level of discourse and understanding, so the objection to dualist terminology goes, that might pre-fix how we come to understand and interpret what we call cognitive phenomena. The theoretic framework called "folk psychology," this objection suggests, is what has perhaps bred the distinction we currently make between the mental and the physical. As science proceeds, the objection continues, the terms we use today that differentiate the mental ("cognitive phenomena") from the neural will on some future day be reducible to the neural. There will no longer be any differentiation. In the final stage, cognitive science, or theory of knowledge, will be the science of neurobiology. The term "mind" will be seen to have been a misnomer for what is a neuro-electric event, a bodily process and nothing else.

Proponents of this view, admirably elucidated by Patricia Churchland's *Neurophysiology*, are not prepared to be dogmatic about this claim.[3] If the percepts we have cannot issue, as we argued, from the body's neural machinery, their reluctance is a seasoned one. In fact, their view will not be able to prevail if what we have argued the empirical facts about neural machinery show prevails. That is, the grounds for distinguishing between neural and mental events derive from an impossibility. It is the impossibility of neural occurrences causing of themselves those events which has led us to come up with the classification "mental." Neural occurrences cannot produce what we have labelled as mental, and it is that which validates the distinction between neural and mental. It is the events themselves that require the distinction. Without the distinction one and the same term, 'neural', would apply equally to a contrary state of affairs. 'Neural' would be that which is momentary, discrete, chaotic, as well as coherent and uniform. One and the same term, however, cannot have contrary meanings for the same event. The features themselves about which we are talking here, e.g., chaotic versus coherent, force the distinction between 'neural' and 'mental'—terms to which the detractors of "folk psychology" object. Our ordinary speech, our "folk parlance," is not the cause of the distinction, the dualism, that objectors to folk psychology's classification believe to be groundless. Folk psychology is grounded in the distinction present in the events themselves in which folk psychology has made the distinction it has. The percept has grounds other than those which neural occurrences can provide.

Since, however, it has been objected that it is not the events themselves but rather the current framework of discourse in which we operate, that has bred the distinction between the neural and the mental, it is useful to examine what those objections are. Churchland has suggested that "folk psychology" may be the cause of our dualistic terminology.

The arguments appear in her chapters entitled "Reduction and the Mind-Body Problem" and "Mental States Irreducible to Neurobiological States?"[4] One argument is that one errs in thinking that only reasons, not causes, induce human behavior.

Man, according to this distinction, is different from other physical entities in that his behavior results from "'a rational-in-the-light-of' relation between the contents of" his "mental states and the content of the decision" to act. Behavior results from a suitable rationale—not causal conditions. Since explanations in the physical sciences are by way of identifying causes, the explanation of human behavior in terms of rationale or reasons is in terms of non-physical relations. This suggests one basis for the distinction between physical and non-physical in the study of human activity.

Churchland argues that the fallacy here is that the behavior of physical bodies and human behavior exhibit such a high degree of similarity that physical causality as explanatory of both may be appropriate. For example, "if a body x has a mass m, and if x suffers a net force of f, then x accelerates at f/m."[5] This is presumably equivalent to the case in which, if I am struck I will move from what is striking me. Since physical causality explains the first condition it can, for Churchland, explain the second, mine. Thus human behavior need not be construed as issuing from reasons or rationales, but simply from causes.

The difficulty with this analysis is that in the first case perception of the relation between being struck and moving is absent, while in the second—my moving—it is not. The similarity Churchland wants, and needs, to have for her argument that it is our current framework of discourse that makes us distinguish between neural and mental is simply not there. Implicit in her argument is the assumption that similarity of behavior implies similarity of kinds in the entities observed. The assumption would be legitimate only if what is observed in a given circumstance is all there is to know about the circumstance and the things involved in it. Two bodies observed to behave in the same way could have their behavior described in the same terms—e.g., in terms of causes only, rather than causes in the one case and reasons or rationale in the other—if what we observe is sufficient for an accurate description. That I *could* void the oncoming body could not be observed, however. Only *I* would think that I could. To an observer from afar I would appear as just another body whose motion in the presence of a mass hitting it is no different from the situation of a mass hitting a body with no capacity (like mine) to move out of the way. While then the description of both events—one body hitting another and a body hitting me—can be put in simply causal terms, causal terms cannot by themselves describe my capacity to sidestep a moving body, since the causal terms are limited to the action of body on body. My motion, assuming I am not hit, cannot, therefore, have causal, exclusively physical, terms in its description. There was not a cause, a body, that made me move. There was a *reason*, that is, the desire to avoid being hit, that made me move when I moved. For Churchland, however, I could never have moved out of the way of the approaching body. Bodily behavior and human behavior differ in ways that require explanations in different terms. The belief that they are equally describable in the same terms, and thus that one can explain human behavior (and thought) in the same terms by which one explains the behavior of physical bodies, collapses a relevant distinction. Churchland's argument does not eliminate the difference between neural and mental.

Nor will it do to suggest that it may be only the limitations of our current scientific understanding that obscures a perfect identity between neurobiology and awareness. Such a suggestion can, of course, be advanced to save *any* hypothesis. Churchland argues that just as it turned out that there is "no such thing as impetus, there may be no such thing as awareness," that "a newer and better theory may yield a theoretically more satisfactory characterization of it." . . . [T]he nature of the representations and their role in that process remain to be empirically discovered by cognitive neurobiology. . . . the notion of a conceptual or theoretical framework is still only roughly delimited and will itself find need to be revised, extended, or perhaps eventually displaced by cognitive neurobiology."[6]

The claim's difficulty lies in the general argument on which it is based, that is, the possible inadequacy of any scientific approach. The specific argument is that it is our current level of scientific understanding that brings us to use the word 'awareness' and what we understand by it. The term (and, with that, the distinction between mental and neural) may be inadequate, however, because the current level of scientific understanding may be inadequate. All things, however, *may* be, unless proven to the contrary. That, though, tells us nothing as a criticism. It merely says that we ought to continue our studies on consciousness to see if certain distinctions can be maintained or, in time, eliminated. That is not a basis for suggesting that current distinctions made in science are valid or invalid, however.

The distinction between mental and neural in "folk psychology" appears also in "property dualism." "Property dualism," simply put, argues this thought experiment: while a blind person conceivably could have all the neurological information that will ever exist about color, a seeing person would still have access to something the blind person did not, that is, the actual experience of color. Accordingly, the neurobiological data and the subjective experience are irreducible one to the other. The data lack what the experience does not. They are two distinct provinces. The neurosciences do not explain fully the perceptual event, implying that the event, therefore, is not wholly neurobiological.[7]

The objection, again from Churchland, to this dualism is twofold; and fails. Churchland argues that "if there are two (at least) modes of knowing about the world, then it is entirely possible that what one knows one knows via a different method. Pregnancy is something one can know about by acquiring the relevant theory from a medical text or by being pregnant. What a childless obstetrician knows about is the very same process as the process known by a pregnant but untutored woman."[8]

If all there is to know about pregnancy via one method is identical to all there is to know via another, actually becoming pregnant, as opposed to a textbook understanding of it, should add nothing to our understanding of it. And that is patently absurd. How would death differ from simply knowing about the bodily processes of mortal decay if Churchland is right? Having a conceptual (textbook) understanding of pregnancy without ever actually having been pregnant is akin to having a concept of a million dollars and then trying to spend it. On Churchland's view, there is no difference between being pregnant and reading about it in a textbook, or knowing about money as opposed to actually having it.

Property dualism contains within it this insight that the thought or study of "X" is not equivalent to the existence "X" or being "X". Knowing and being are different: knowing pregnant and being pregnant are different. Thus with regard to money: it is inarguable that all my conceptualization about money will matter nothing at my local grocery if I have none with which to buy the loaf of bread I want.

Churchland's comparison, then, is ineffective. You must become pregnant to know what it is to become pregnant. Thus, any method that does not involve actually becoming pregnant cannot be identical to a method—such as obstetrical science—by means of which one does not become pregnant. All there is to know via one method is not all there is to know via another.

Along the same lines, knowing that, e.g., red is a certain gamma state in one's o patterns, Churchland's second objection[9] does not equate, contrary to what she maintains, with the percept "red." Otherwise, each time I think that way about red I would have the percept red. It is in no wise, therefore, to beg the question, as Churchland thinks it is, to say the percept "red" differs from a neurophysiological account of it. There is an actual case why the percept "red" is not identifiable with a neurophysiological account, as just noted. Knowledge of the entire neural network involved in the event "redness" does not equate with "redness." The full knowledge of "X" requires more than the knowledge of how it comes about or registers quantitatively on a neural chromatometer. The difference checks Churchland's objection: an experience is not identical with its description or account.

The argument about the difference between full knowledge and knowledge of how a thing comes about is important in addressing the criticism of "folk psychology." The criticism holds that once all neurological data are in hand our way of speaking about "mental events" will be corrected such that the expression "mental events" will cease to have a function in respected science. This is the view Churchland represents. Implicit in the view is that no data will be remaining that could overturn the neurobiological science's dismissal of the expression "mental events." The neural event and the data will have to be reducible to one another; for if anything is left over or remaining, it could exist to overturn the new neuroscience's dismissal of the expression "mental event." There is no basis, though, that establishes that once all possible neurological data are obtained the expression "mental event" will thereby cease to have meaning or refer to something non-neurological. That it will, though, is what has to be proven if one wishes to hold that the complete acquisition of neurological data will end our belief in the term "mental event," the reference to the non-physical.

Property dualism, to explain it otherwise, does not show that percepts are not neurobiological in cause and structure. One cannot argue that the difference between "knowledge how" and "full knowledge" says anything about how the data that are known come to be known. What a property dualism does show, nevertheless, is that the criticism of "folk psychology" as being responsible for the dualism of mental versus material is not necessarily an invalidating criticism of the dualism. For no neurobiological science will be able to claim an absoluteness or totality of data such as to discredit or render obsolete the theoretic framework embedded in "folk psychology." The irreducible difference between experience and "know-how" (book understanding) shows that neurobiological science cannot lay claim to the totality of data about any event of consciousness. Some datum or data will always be remaining, as in the actual experience, which will not be reducible to its scientific description or account. On Churchland's own grounds, such totality of data is required if the data and the neural event are ever to be proven as reducible to one another. Property dualism, in bringing this to light, negates the Churchland criticism of "folk psychology's" distinction between mental and neural.

The grounds for difference between the percept and neurobiological states/events reside in the causal inability of neurological mechanisms to suffice for perceptual states. Does this means, then, that certain non-human awareness has a basis irreducible to the neural? At the level of the higher primates where the percept is sufficiently complicated and integral is it the case that their awareness is transmaterial? Surely there is no way of knowing, for we have no ability to share their percepts. There is no way we could plot our percept upon theirs and see if they matched. In point of content, our access to their percepts is limited to how we see such primates behave in reaction to a stimulus. But here what we would infer their percept to be could only at best be through some comparison with what ours would be in the presence of the same stimulus. The comparison would be an exercise in conjecture at best, as therefore would be any judgment on the animal's transmaterial status.

One other issue remains. If man evolved from a lower complexity (on this hypothesis he was originally, like all other beings in the universe, undifferentiated from the *Urstoff* itself), how did he, in that evolution, become immaterial? The original stuff of the universe, which has developed into all the complexities of material existence today, according to the evolutionary hypothesis, was not immaterial, after all. If he is not a product of evolution, how is it that, in a universe of matter, man is immaterial? Both questions are pointing to an order of existence not identified with matter. They appear to indicate the need for an intervention from that order to account for the immateriality we have argued the activity of thought (concept formation) and consciousness shows man must have.

Here one should probably simply comment that one should let the evidence speak for itself. Wherever it leads the conclusion should be left standing. In a universe that is patently material, an immaterial efficacy within it requires an explanation that is not of the universe. Matter cannot evolve into non-matter; matter cannot make something non-matter. There is nothing untoward in moving to the suggestion, then, that an immaterial existence must have a rôle in causing human immateriality. If the generality of our concepts preclude in them a material component, and if consciousness cannot be reduced to neural activity, the suggestion has a merit not unlike that in other situations where evidence has been the cause of the suggestion.

NOTES

1. The literature on reincarnation is vast, and interpretation/commentaries on it differing. I have tried to present those notions common throughout or compatible with what has been understood as reincarnation doctrine. Part of the difficulty in such an undertaking is identifying correctly spokesmen for reincarnation, the explanations about reincarnation being so various. In any case, I do view the core of reincarnation belief to be the doctrine of past lives, and that is why I have chosen to address it from this angle.

The most readable treatment I have come across on reincarnation is Hans Ten Dam, *Exploring Reincarnation*, (New York: Arkana/Viking Penguin, 1990). Other works are Patricia Blakiston, *The Pre-existence and Transmigration of Souls*, (London: Regency, 1970), C. W. Ducasse, *A Critical Examination of the Belief in Life After Death*, (Springfield: Thomas, 1960), Joe Fisher, *The Case For Reincarnation*, (London: Grafton Books, 1986), Joseph Read and S. L. Cranston, *Reincarnation: The Phoenix Fire Mystery*, (New York: Julian Press, Crown Publishers, 1977), Hans Holzer, *Life Beyond Life: the Evidence for Reincarnation*, (West Nyack, NY: Parker, 1985), J. M. E. McTaggart, *Human Immortality and Pre-Existence*, (New York: Kraus, 1970), Wendy D. O'Flaherty (ed.), *Karma and Rebirth in Classical Indian Traditions*, (Berkeley, CA: University of California Press, 1980), Ian Stevenson, *Twenty Cases Suggestive of Reincarnation*, (New York: American Society for Psychical Research, 1966).

2. Even *in extremis* were percepts held to be reducible to neuro-electric states they still could never be in contact with one another. As neuro-electric events they would be limited, one would think, to following upon each other just as flashes of lightning do. The instantaneousness of neuro-electric events preclude contact among them inasmuch as contact requires the existence long enough of something so that something else can come next to it.

3. Patricia Smith Churchland, *Neurophilosophy: Toward a Unified Science of the Mind/Brain*, (Cambridge, MA: M.I.T. Press, 1989), pp. 288–303.

4. *Ibid.*, pp. 277–347.

5. *Ibid.*, p. 305. This distinction between causes and reasons appears in pp. 303–05.

6. *Ibid.*, pp. 309–10. Strictly speaking, Churchland should not use the adjective 'cognitive' since its usage seems implicitly to admit of a difference from

neurobiological. Neural event (the neurobiological) and knowledge (experience) should mean the same in Churchland's perfect science, such that "knowledge" ceases to be a working category in an accurate and full understanding of the neurobiological. In that science "neurobiological" will convey always what the terms "cognitive" and "experiential" do today and "neural event" what "knowledge" and "experience" do currently. In Churchland's thesis the words 'knowledge', 'cognitive' 'understanding' 'experience' 'experiential' and the difference from the material/neuro-electric to which they refer will cease to exist. Human science will advance to that point where future discourse will not contain words that indicate a non-material basis of any event that is currently referred to by the term 'knowledge' and its like.

7. *Ibid.*, pp. 330–34.
8. *Ibid.*, p. 332.
9. *Ibid.*, p. 333.

BIBLIOGRAPHY

Adams, R. D. and M. Victor. *Principles of Neurology* (2nd ed'n.). (New York: McGraw Hill, 1981).

Addison, J. T. *Life Beyond Death in the Beliefs of Mankind.* (Boston: Houghton Mifflin, 1932).

Aquinas, Thomas. *Basic Writings,* Anton Pegis (ed.) (New York: Random House, 1945, 2 vols.)

———. *On Being and Essence.* Trans. by Joseph Bobick. (Notre Dame, IN: University of Notre Dame. 1965).

Aquinas, Thomas. *Truth,* trans. by Robert W. Mulligan. (Chicago: Henry Regnery, 1952).

Aristotle. *Physics.* Trans. with commentary by W. D. Ross. (New York: Oxford University Press, 1966).

Atwater, P. M. H. *Coming Back to Life: The After-Effects of the Near-Death Experience.* (New York: Dodd, Mead, 1988).

Barbizet, Jacques. *Human Memory and Its Pathology,* trans. by D. Jardine. (San Francisco: W. H. Freeman, 1970).

Barrett, Sir William. *Death-Bed Visions: The Psychical Experience of the Dying.* (North Hampshire, England: Aquarian Press, 1986).

Bayless, Raymond. *Apparitions and Survival of Death.* (New York: Citadel Press, 1973).

Berger, T. W. and R. F. Thompson. "Identification of Pyramidal Cells as the Critical Elements in Hippocampal Neuronal Plasticity During Learning". National Academy of Sciences of the United States of America. *Proceedings. Biological Sciences.* (75), 1572–76, 1978.

Berkeley, George. *Principles of Human Knowledge.* (New York: Bobbs-Merrill, 1970).

Blackiston, Patricia. *The Pre-Existence and Transmigration of Souls.* (London: Regency, 1970).

Blackmore, Susan J. *Beyond the Body: An Investigation of Out-of-the-Body Experiences.* (London: Heinemann, 1982).

Blakemore, Colin. *Mechanics of the Mind.* (Cambridge: Cambridge University Press, 1977).

Bohm, David. *Wholeness and the Implicate Order.* (London: Routledge & Kegan Paul, 1980).

Bolzano, Bernard. *Paradoxes of the Infinite,* trans. by D. A. Steele (London: Routledge & Kegan Paul, 1950).

Boyer, Carl. *A History of Mathematics.* (Princeton, NJ: Princeton University Press, 1985).

Brinkley, Dannion, with Paul Perry. *Saved by the Light.* (New York: Harper Paperbacks, 1994).

Broad, C. D. *Lectures on Psychical Research.* (London: Routledge & Kegan Paul, 1962).

_____. *The Mind and Its Place in Nature.* (New York: Harcourt, Brace, 1929).

Bunge, Richard. "Glial Cells and the Central Myelin Sheath". *Physiological Review* (1968), 197–251.

Carpenter, Malcolm, *Human Neuroanatomy.* 7th ed'n. (Baltimore, MD: Williams and Wilkins, 1976).

Churchland, Patricia Smith. *Neurophilosophy: Toward a Unified Science of the Mind-Brain.* (Cambridge, MA: M.I.T. Press, 1986).

_____. "The Timing of Sensation: Reply to Libet." *Philosophy of Science,* 48 (1981), 492–97.

Churchland, Paul M. *Matter and Consciousness: A Contemporary Introduction to the Philosophy of Mind.* (Cambridge, MA: M.I.T. Press, 1988, Revised ed'n.

Cooper, J. R., F. E. Bloom, and R. H. Roth. *The Biochemical Basis of Neuropharmacology.* 2nd ed'n. (New York: Oxford University Press, 1982).

Cordaro, L. and Ison, J. R. "Observer Bias in Classical Conditioning of the Planaria." *Psychological Reports* 13 (1963), 787–89.

Coyle, J. T., D. L. Price, and M. R. De Long. "Alzheimer's Disease: A Disorder of Cortical Cholinergic Innervation." *Science* 219 (1983), 1184–90.

Dempsey, David. *The Way We Die: An Investigation of Death and Dying in America Today.* (New York: McGraw Hill, 1977).

Dennett, Daniel C. "Can Machines Think?" in *How We Know,* ed. M. Shafto. (San Francisco: Harper & Row, 1986, pp. 1–26, 99.

_____. *Consciousness Explained.* (Boston, MA: Little, Brown, 1991).

Descartes, René. *Meditations on First Philosophy* in *The Philosophical Works of Descartes,* trans. by E. S. Haldane and G. R. T. Ross. (Cambridge: Cambridge University Press, 1973), vol. 1.

Dodds, E. R. "Why I Do Not Believe in Survival." *Proceedings of the Society for Psychical Research.* London 42(1934), 147–72.

Donchin, E. "Brain Electrical Correlates of Pattern Recognition" in *International Symposium on Signal Analysis and Pattern Recognition in Biomedical Engineering,* ed. G. F. Inbar. (New York: Wiley, 1975), pp. 199–218.

Doore, Gary (ed.). *What Survives? Contemporary Explorations of Life After Death.* (Los Angeles: Jeremy Tarcher, 1990).

Ducasse, C. J. *A Critical Examination of the Belief in Life After Death.* (Springfield, IL: Charles C. Thomas, 1961).

Ebom, Martin. *The Evidence for Life After Death.* (New York: Signet, 1977).

Eccles, Sir John (ed.). *Brain and Conscious Experience.* (New York: Springer Verlag, 1966).

_____. *The Human Psyche.* (New York: Springer International, 1980).

_____. *The Understanding of the Brain.* (New York: McGraw-Hill, 1973).

Ettinger, Robert C. W. *The Prospect of Immortality.* (Garden City, NY: Doubleday, 1964).

Everett, N. B. *Functional Neuroanatomy* (6th ed'n.) (Philadelphia: Lea and Febiger, 1973).

Flanagan, Owen J., Jr. *The Science of the Mind.* (Cambridge, MA: M.I.T. Press, 1984).

Fosdick, Harry Emerson. *The Assurance of Immortality.* (New York: Macmillan, 1914).

Gallup, George, Jr. (with William Proctor). *Adventures In Immortality: A Look Beyond the Threshold of Death.* (New York: McGraw-Hill, 1982).

Freed, W. J. "Functional Brain Tissue Transplantation: Reversal of Lesion-induced Rotation by Intraventricular Substantia Nigra and Adrenal Medulla Grafts, with a Note on Intracranial Retinal Grafts." *Biological Psychiatry* 18/11, (1983) 1205–67.

Grey, Margot. *Return from Death: An Exploration of the Near-Death Experience.* (London: Arkana, 1985).

Greyson, Bruce. "A Typology of Near-Death Experiences." *American Journal of Psychiatry*, 142 (August 1985), 967–69.

————. "Near-Death Experiences and Attempted Suicide." *Suicide and Life-Threatening Behavior*, 11 (1981), 101–16.

Grosso, Michael. "Towards an Exploration of Near-Death Phenomena." *Journal of the American Society for Psychical Research*, 75 (1981), 37–60.

Groz, Anton, "The Place Between: Ancient Tibetan Explanations for Death-Return Experiences." *The Quest* 2/4(1989), 60–69.

Guardini, Romano. *The Last Things*, translated by C. E. Forsyth and G. B. Branham. (New York: Pantheon Books, 1954).

Hancock, Harry N. *And After This?* (New York: Longmans, Green, 1954).

Head, Joseph & S. I. Cranston. *Reincarnation: An East-West Anthology.* (Wheaton, IL: Quest, 1985).

Herbert, Nick. *Quantum Reality.* (New York: Anchor Books, 1987).

Hick, John. *Death and Eternal Life.* (New York: Harper & Row, 1976).

Hillman, James. *Suicide and the Soul.* (New York: Harper & Row, 1965).

Hillyard, S. A., & M. Kutas. "Electrophysiology of Cognitive Processing." *Annual Review of Psychology* 34, (1983), 33–61.

Holzer, Hans. *Life Beyond Death: The Evidence for Reincarnation.* (West Nyack, NY: Parker, 1985).

Hume, David. *A Treatise of Human Nature*, L. A. Selby-Biggs, (ed.) (London: Oxford University Press, 1968).

Huxley, Aldous. *The Doors of Perception* and *Heaven and Hell.* (New York: Harper & Row, 1956).

James, William. *The Will to Believe* and *Human Immortality.* (New York: Dover, 1959).

Kandel, Eric R. *Cellular Basis of Behavior: An Introduction to Behavioral Neurobiology.* (San Francisco: W. H. Freeman, 1976).

Kant, Immanuel. *Critique of Pure Reason,* trans. by Norman Kemp Smith. (New York: St. Martin's Press, 1965).

Kastenbaum, Robert. *Is There Life After Death?* (New York: Prentice-Hall, 1984).

Kelsey, Morton. *After Life: The Other Side of Dying.* (New York: Crossroad, 1982).

Kety, S. S. "The Biological Roots of Mental Illness: Their Ramifications Through Central Metabolism, Synaptic Activity, Genetics, and the Environment. *Harvard Lecture* 71, (1978)1–22.

Kosestenbau, Peter. *Is There An Answer to Death?* (Englewood Cliffs, NJ: Prentice-Hall, 1984).

Kolata, G. "New Neurons Form in Adulthood." *Science* 224(1984), 1325–26.

Krieger, D. T. & J. B. Martin. "Brain Peptides," *New England Journal of Medicine* 305:15 (April 9, 1981), 876–85.

Kubler-Ross, Elizabeth. *On Death and Dying.* (London: Tavistock, 1973).

Kuffler, S. W., J. J. Nicholls, & A. R. Martin. *From Neurons to Brain: A Cellular Approach to the Functions of the Nervous System.* 2nd ed'n. (Sunderland, MA: Sinauer, 1984).

Lamont, C. *The Illusion of Immortality.* (New York: Philosophical Library, 1950).

Levin, Robert. "Is Your Brain Really Necessary?" *Science*. 210 (1980), 1232–34.

Libet, Benjamin. "The Experimental Evidence for Subjective Referral of a Sensory Experience Backwards in Time: Reply to P. S. Churchland." *Philosophy of Science*, 48 (1981), 182–97.

_____. "Subjectivity Antedating of a Sensory Experience and Mind-Brain Theories." *Journal of Theoretical Biology*, 114 (1985), 563–70.

_____. "The Timing of a Subjective Experience." *Behavioral and Brain Science*, 12 (1989), 183–85.

Lorimer, David. *Survival? Body, Mind, and Death in the Light of Psychic Experience.* (London: Routledge & Kegan Paul, 1984).

Lulianowicz, A. "Autoscopic Phenomena." *Archives of Neurology and Psychiatry*. American Medical Association, vol. 80 (August 1958), 199.

Lund, David H. *Perception, Mind and Personal Identity: A Critique of Materialism.* (Lanham, MD: University Press of America, 1994).

Luria, A. R. *The Working Brain: An Introduction to Neuropsychology*, trans. by Basil Haigh. (New York: Basic Books, 1973).

Lynch, Gary, James T. McGaugh, and Norman M. Weinberger (eds.). *Neurobiology of Learning and Memory.* (New York: Guilford, 1984).

Margolis, Joseph. *Persons and Minds: The Prospects of Non-reductive Materialism.* (Dordrect, Holland: D. Reidel, 1978).

Maritain, Jacques. *Man's Destiny in Eternity.* (Boston, MA: Beacon Press, 1949).

Marsh, Michael. A *Matter of Personal Survival: Life After Death.* (Wheaton, IL: Quest, 1985).

Martin, W. "Waiting for the End." *The Atlantic Monthly.* (June 1982), 31–37.

McAdams, Elizabeth E. & Raymond Bayless. *The Case For Life After Death: Parapsychologists Look at the Evidence.* (Chicago: Nelson Hall, 1981).

McEwen, Bruce S. "Interaction Between Hormones and Nervous Tissues." *Scientific American.* 235/1 1976, 48–58.

McTaggart, James M. E. *Human Immortality and Pre-Existence.* (New York: Kraus, 1970).

Moody, Raymond, Jr. *Life After Life.* (Convington, GA: Mockingbird Books, 1975).

_____. *The Light Beyond.* (New York: Bantam, 1988).

Monroe, Robert. *Far Journeys.* (Garden City, NJ: Doubleday, 1985).

_____. *Journeys Out of the Body.* (Garden City, NJ: Anchor Books, 1977).

Morse, Melvin (with Paul Perry). *Closer to the Light.* (New York: Villard, 1992).

Myers, F. W. H. *Human Personality and its Survival of Bodily Death.* 2 vols. (London: Longmans Green, 1903).

Myers, R. E., & R. W. Sperry. "Interhemispheric Communication Through the Corpus Callosum: Mnemonic Carry-over Between the Hemispheres." *Archives of Neurology and Psychiatry* 80(1958) 298–303.

Oakley, D. A. (ed.). *Brain and Mind.* (New York: Methuen, 1985).

O'Flaherty, Wendy (ed.). *Karma and Rebirth in Classical Indian Tradition.* (Berkeley, CA: University of California Press, 1980).

Ojermahn, George A. "Brain Organization for Language from the Perspective of Electrical Stimulation Mapping." *Behavioral and Brain Sciences* 612, (1983), 189–230.

Osis, Karl and Erlendur Haroldsson. *At the Hour of Death.* Revised ed'n. (New York: Hastings House, 1986).

_____. & J. L. Mitchell. "Physiological Correlates of Reported Out-of-Body Experiences." *Journal of the Society for Psychical Research,* 49 (1977), 424–36.

Penfield, Wilder. *The Mystery of the Mind.* (Princeton, NJ: Princeton University Press, 1975).

_____. & Phanor Perot. "The Brain's Record of Auditory and Visual Experience: A Final Summary and Discussion" *Brain,* 86 (December 1963), 595–696.

Penrose, Roger. *The Emperor's New Mind.* (New York: Oxford University Press, 1989).

Perry, Elaine K., & Robert H. Perry, "The Cholinergic System in Alzheimer's Disease." *Trends in Neuroscience* (1982) 261–72.

Plato. *Plato's Phaedo,* trans. by R. S. Bluck. (New York: Bobbs-Merrill, 1955).

Popper, Karl R. & John C. Eccles. *The Self and Its Brain; An Argument for Interaction.* (New York: Springer International, 1977). Parts I, II, & III.

Pribam, K. H. "Holographic Memory" (Interview). *Psychology Today,* 12, (1979), 70–84.

_____. "The Neurophysiology of Remembering." *Scientific American* 220/1, (1969) 73–80.

Price, H. H. "Survival and the Idea of Another World." *Proceedings of the Society for Psychical Research,* London, 50 (1952).

Rawlings, Maurice. *Beyond Death's Door.* (Nashville, TN: Thomas Nelson, 1978).

Read, Joseph, & S. L. Cranston. *Reincarnation: The Phoenix Fire Mystery.* (New York: Julian Press, Crown Publishers, 1977).

Ring, Kenneth. *Heading Towards Omega.* (New York: Harper & Row, 1982).

_____. *Life at Death. A Scientific Investigation of the Near-Death Experience.* (New York: Coward, McGann and Geoghegan, 1980).

_____. & S. Franklin. "Do Suicide Survivors Report Near-Death Experiences?" *Omega* 12 (1991–92), 191–200.

Rogo, D. Scott. *Life After Death: The Case for Survival of Bodily Death.* (Guilford, Surrey: Aquarian Press, 1986).

Rose, Steven. *The Conscious Brain.* (New York: Alfred Knopf, 1973).

Rumelhart, David E. & James T. McLelland. *Parallel Distributed Processing: Explorations in the Microstructure of Cognition.* Vol. 1: Foundations. (Cambridge, MA: M.I.T. Press, 1986).

Sabom, Michael. *Recollections of Death: A Medical Investigation.* (New York: Harper & Row, 1982).

Schmitt, F. O., F. G. Worden, G. Adelman, and S. G. Dennis (eds.). *The Organization of the Cerebral Cortex.* (Cambridge, MA: M.I.T. Press, 1981).

Shepherd, Gordon M. *Neurobiology.* (New York: Oxford University Press, 1983).

Smith, C. U. M. *The Brain: Towards An Understanding.* (New York: Putnam, 1970).

Snyder, Solomon H. "The Dopamine Hypothesis of Schizophrenia: Focus on the Dopamine Receptor." *Journal of American Psychiatry* 133 (1976) 197–202.

Sperry, R. W. "Mental Phenomena and Causal Determinants in Brain Function," in *Consciousness and the Brain,* G. Globus, G. Maxwell, and I. Savodnik (eds.). (New York: Plenum, 1976), pp. 163–77.

Stevenson, Ian. *Twenty Cases Suggestive of Reincarnation.* 2nd ed'n. (Charlottesville, VA: University Press of Virginia, 1974).

_____. *Cases of the Reincarnation Type,* vol. 1, *Ten Cases in India.* (Charlottesville, VA: University Press of Virginia, 1975).

_____. *Cases of the Reincarnation Type*, vol. 2. *Ten Cases in Sri Lanka.* (Charlottes-
ville, VA: University Press of Virginia, 1975).

Sutherland, Cherie. *Reborn in the Light: Life after Near-Death Experiences.* (New
York: Bantam Books, 1992).

Swinburne, Richard. *The Evolution of the Soul.* (New York: Oxford University
Press, 1986).

TenDam, Hans. *Exploring Reincarnation*, trans. by A. E. J. Wills. (London: Arkana,
1990).

Thouless, Robert H. "Do We Survive Bodily Death?" *Proceedings of the Society for
Psychical Research*, 57, (October, 1984) 213.

Twemlow, S., G. Gabbard, and Jones, F. "The Out-of-Body Experience: A
Phenomenological Typology Based on Questionnaire Responses." *American
Journal of Psychiatry* 139 (1982), 450–55.

Trevarthen, C. "Experimental Evidence for a Brain Stem Contribution to Visual
Perception in Man." *Brain, Behaviour, and Evolution* 3 (1970) 338–53.

Weatherhead, Leslie D. *After Death.* (Nashville, TN: Abingdon Press, n.d.).

Weber, Renée. *Dialogues with Scientists and Sages.* (New York: Routledge & Kegan
Paul, 1986).

Wilson, Colin. *Afterlife.* (London: Harrap, 1985).

Wilson, D. H., A. G. Reeves, M. S. Gazaniga, and C. Culver. "Cerebral
Commisnurotomy for the Control of Intractable Seizures." *Neurology* 27
(1977), 708–15.

Winlow, William & Rudolf Markstein (eds.). *The Neurobiology of Dopamine Systems.*
(Exeter, England: Manchester University Press, 1986).

Young, J. Z. *Philosophy and the Brain.* (New York: Oxford University Press, 1988).

Zaleski, Carol. *Otherworld Journeys.* (New York: Oxford University Press, 1987).

This book was typeset
by
Craig W. O'Dell
in 11-point Baskerville on 13 points of lead.
[John Baskerville, English type-designer, b. 1706, d. 1775.]
DATASET, BLOOMINGTON, ILLINOIS
